Bargain Junkie

LIVING the GOOD LIFE on the CHEAP

BY ANNIE KORZEN

09 10 11 12 13 RR2 10 9 8 7 6 5 4 3 2

ISBN-13: 978-1522810988
ISBN-10: 1522810986

An earlier version of A FRUGALISTA'S REVENGE appeared in the *New York Times*.

An earlier version of I GO ON *OPRAH*, OR, A FRUGALISTA REGRETS appeared in the *Jewish Journal of Los Angeles*.

An earlier version of IT'S A NOT-SO-WONDERFUL LIFE appeared in the *Los Angeles Times*.

www.AnnieKorzen.com

To Benni, for everything.

Contents

CONTENTS

CONTENTS

Acknowledgment

I guess I have to thank my friend and agent, Julia Lord, for badgering me into writing this book—even though she knows how much I hate to work.

Introduction

The market goes up, the market goes down. We're in a boom, we're in a recession, we're in a depression. We're told to "live richly," we're told to "spend cautiously." None of this economic see-saw has ever affected me because I've been a thriftaholic all my life.

I was brought up in a Bronx railroad flat by poor immigrants. My mother would use a tea bag, then squeeze it dry, hang it up, and use it again the next day: I hated her for this. My father was a tailor, and he made all my clothes: I hated him for this.

I wanted to live like my friends, with spacious homes, trendy outfits, and all the other trappings of middle-class American life. Most of all, I wanted fresh tea bags. I enjoy those pleasures now, but I have learned to respect my parents' frugality.

I rarely buy anything that hasn't been pre-worn, pre-used, or pre-loved. I'm such a compulsive reuser that when I'm in a restaurant and see the anorexic girl at the next table leaving a pile of food on her plate I have to fight the impulse to say, "Excuse me, but if you're not going to finish that, would you mind passing it this way?"

My thrifty (thrifty, not stingy; stingy is nasty) lifestyle has allowed me to have a comfy home filled with objects of value (the most valuable object being my Danish husband, Benni, and he was also pre-loved; I would never get a husband retail). I've also managed to educate my child, travel all over the world, and give the occasional dinner party. I try not to do this last one too often. If God had wanted people to cook, she wouldn't have invented restaurants.

What my bargainista philosophy has not allowed me to do is to own a $150,000 Birkin crocodile and diamond bag, or even a measly low-end $9,000 Birkin bag. Somehow, I don't feel I've missed much. I'm perfectly happy with my lightweight, washable, silver Sportsac. I got it on eBay for twelve bucks.

Acquiring Stuff

$1 Things Don't Really Make Us Happy—Or So They Say

They've done some scientific studies recently on the causes of happiness. (I guess they're looking for a cure.) It seems that it doesn't come from wealth or celebrity. Happiness comes from spending time with friends and family: people you care about and who care about you. Personally, I'd rather be rich and famous, and while I'm waiting for that to happen I'm lucky enough to have a lot of love in my life. But luv, shmuv: my name is Annie, and I'm a shopaholic.

Years ago, I was at a dinner party in New York and I was talking to Garrison Keillor's then-wife. She was Danish, and she told me how insulted she was that her new American friends invited her to go shopping. "Shopping? Why? Is there something wrong with the way I dress?" Poor dear. This no-nonsense, sensible Scandinavian didn't understand that for some of us shopping is a form of recreation— even of meditation. I wander through the racks, I feel the fabrics, I study the price tags, I reach Nirvana.

I guess shopping fills some emptiness in me that I'm not even aware of. I'm happiest when I come home with bags full of knit tops, vintage jewelry, antique linens, whatever. My dresser is crammed, my closets are stuffed, and my rooms are filled to the brim with artsy collectibles and rare first editions. Being surrounded by stuff gives me a feeling of security. I could never be comfortable in a bare, spare, stark environment. Empty spaces give me the creeps, and so do the

THINGS YOU'LL NEVER HEAR ME SAY

• "I have to have it, no matter what it costs."

• "I couldn't possibly wear that. It's last year's style!"

• "You get what you pay for."

• "He who dies with the most toys wins."

• "I can't wait for the big game. What time is it on?"

This last one has nothing to do with thrifty living. It's just something you'll never hear me say.

people who live in them. Minimalists tend not to have warm and huggy personalities.

There's just one little problem: I have no money. Somehow I managed to get through the booming '80s and the rockin' '90s without stocks, bonds, real estate, or a 401(k). Maybe that's because I've never had a real job. I've only worked at fun things like acting, writing, performing solo shows, mothering, and nap-taking—not a good way to build an investment portfolio. But I discovered that you don't have to break the bank to live a good life. Read on!

Bargainista Fashionista

Have you ever noticed how frumpy some rich women are? I'm thinking Barbara Bush. I'm thinking Margaret Thatcher. I'm thinking Queen Elizabeth. Well, it's no accident; it's deliberate. Someone from a ritzy old-money family explained to me, "Being fashionable shows lack of character." So now, when I meet some nouveau Beverly Hills type dressed head to toe in Prada-Yada-Yada, I think to myself, "Aha, she lacks character." And the funny thing is, it usually turns out to be true.

Well, I think I have character, but I'm not rich enough to aspire to frumpiness. Sure, I have my dowdy moments of elastic-waist pants and socks with sandals. But I also lust after pretty, stylish things. Lots of them. Here's how I find them—for next to no money.

YARD, TAG, AND GARAGE SALES

My addiction began when we moved from New York to Los Angeles. We were invited to our first big-time Hollywood party. There were going to be celebs at this event, and I needed something glitzy. On my way to Loehmann's in Beverly Hills, I passed by a yard sale and found this fabulous Lillie Rubin jacket covered in sparkly red sequins and beads. The price was twenty bucks, and that's when I decided I would never buy retail again.

Unfortunately, I hadn't yet learned that L.A. is the land of the casual. They're so laid back they don't even pronounce the whole word: It's the land of the caszzz. The party turned out to be an informal barbecue. All the skinny blondes were in jeans. I was a sparkly, sequined idiot, but it was too late: I had been bitten by the second-hand bug and have never recovered.

There are actually two different kinds of yard sales. One is the private person who is moving, empty nesting, spring cleaning, whatever. You can find plenty of good stuff here, but it's catch-as-catch-can. If you're willing to wade through disorganized piles of worthless crap—which I am—you might find one great item. I just scored a quilted silk jacket for fifty cents. It was reversible, so you could say I bought two jackets for a quarter each.

On Thursday I start checking the ads in the *L.A. Times*, Craigslist, *The PennySaver*, and our local neighborhood weekly. I can often tell from the ad if the sale is right for me. If they feature kids' stuff or surfboards, I stay away. (But when my Danish sister-in-law visits, we check out these places, and she finds tons of new toys for her grandchildren in Copenhagen.) By Saturday morning, I've compiled my list, I put the first address into the GPS, and we're off and running.

I'm happiest when a whole block or entire neighborhood does a group sale and I can just stroll from house to house, getting landscaping ideas as I examine the goodies.

Even urban areas are catching on to the tag sale phenomenon. There are no garages or front lawns, but people are inventive. I've been to "stoop sales" in Brooklyn where people sell their stuff from the front steps of their apartment building while they enjoy their morning Danish and *The Sunday Times*.

ESTATE SALES

These are the upscale cousins of the yard sale. They are usually well organized by a pro who has been hired to liquidate the possessions of a deceased person. Since I'm on the hunt for vintage clothing and jewelry, and my husband collects rare books, we like buying from dead people. These two- or three-day events can be pricier than ordinary yard sales, so I tend to go on the last day, when things are usually half-off.

My husband, Benni, is Danish, and just like the ex–Mrs. Keillor, he hates to shop. I pick up stuff for him when I can, but certain things need to be tried on. Benni needed a suit, and I saw an ad that the *Boston Legal* wardrobe department was getting rid of its inventory. I dragged him to the sale with the promise that if he bought some clothes I would go with him to one of those brainless Hollywood comedies made for prepubescent boys of all ages. It was a fair trade: I almost laughed at least twice during the movie, and Benni now proudly sports his Zegna suit ($120) and Hugo Boss jacket ($40). The jacket even has a name written on the label: James Spader.

I walked into one such sale, and they had a basket of sunglasses for five dollars each. The lenses were scratched and useless, but the frames were by designers such as Versace, Armani, and Prada. I bought them all and had the lenses replaced with my prescription. Clever, yes?

THE SCHMOOZE FACTOR

Besides saving heaps of money, enjoying the thrill of the hunt, and exploring some beautiful homes, there's another reason I love yard sales: the social aspect. I come from New York, where strangers speak to each other all the time. They chit-chat at the theater box office, they converse in the apartment building elevator, and they form alliances in the dog run at the park. I have a friend who met her husband on the subway. She started talking to him when she noticed he was reading a novel she loved. New Yorkers have gotten a bum rap as being cold, but they are actually the friendliest people in the world (unless you irritate them, in which case they will curse you *and* your mother).

Moving to L.A. was a big culture shock for me. Besides the unspeakable horror of blueberry bagels, there's the isolation of the car culture. I desperately missed the person-to-person contact of the Big Apple. The social activity of yard sales was a lifesaver.

I've met some fascinating characters, like the ninety-four-year-old TV comedy writer who has a new joke every time we run into him, or the white-turbaned Sikh couple who deal in contemporary art. There was one sale run by two gay furniture designers who offered every buyer a glass of champagne. Try to get that at Bloomingdale's!

I also appreciate getting personal information about an object before I purchase it. One day I spotted a beautiful vintage lace bridal veil that I considered buying for my son's fiancée, Alisa. The seller and I were having a fine old time comparing wedding notes until she said, "Yes, the event was fabulous. Too bad the marriage only lasted eight months." I am usually not a superstitious person, but I decided not to buy the veil, just in case there really is such a thing as karma.

THE CHURCH, SCHOOL, OR CHARITY RUMMAGE SALE

It's large, it's varied, and prices are rock-bottom. Plus, the money will hopefully be used for a good cause. I say "hopefully" because not every cause is equally dear to my heart. When I questioned the high price of some beat-up Uggs, one lady said, "But it's for charity!" The charity in question was something like the Toy Poodle Society. Not at the top of my must-give-to list.

Like estate sales, rummage sales have special deals on the second day, when they just want to get rid of everything. I walked into a church event last week and they said, "Fill a bag for a dollar." I filled three bags with Bjørn clogs, red lizard Western boots, an Eileen Fisher knit top, and the brand-new striped number that I'm wearing on the book cover. Just so you don't think I'm too greedy, I give away much of this loot to friends and family. And when I realize that I still bought too much, I donate it to my thrift store or just leave it atop public trash containers for the homeless. Greedy, yes. Wasteful, no.

THRIFT SHOPS: USED IS THE NEW BLACK

I've seen TV actresses and models prowling the racks at Goodwill. Most thrift stores have regular sales, senior discounts, and two-for-one days. My fave is a chain in California and Florida called Out of the Closet. The proceeds go toward helping people with AIDS. (By the way, the Alaska "Out of the Closet" Sarah Palin favors is not a thrift shop; it is a for-profit consignment shop that was illegally infringing on the real Out of the Closet's registered trademark.)

Every Sunday at Out of the Closet, many items are reduced to one dollar. Needless to say, I shop there only on Sundays. I get there when the doors open at ten, because the competition is fierce. Here are some of my one-buck treasures:

- Ralph Lauren black velvet evening trousers, which I paired with a Harari silk top when hosting my son's engagement party.

- A Diane von Furstenberg floral wrap dress, which I've used so many times that by now each wearing costs about a nickel.

- Zillions of CP Shades separates for those comfy, frumpy, but still a-little-pretty days.

- A 1950s smoky mauve lace cocktail dress. I'm still waiting for the right occasion to wiggle into this hot little number. I may have to lose 20 pounds first—and pull in my tummy with the Spanx I bought on eBay.

- A Wilson's tan suede blazer for Benni. First time out, he managed to dip his sleeve into a bowl of tomato soup, but at these prices, who cares? Dollar clothing gives new meaning to the phrase "Easy come, easy go."

And, depending on the salesperson, they sometimes add a 10 percent senior discount. I'm serious: ninety cents for a suede jacket. I am a bargainista genius!

HOSPITAL AND CHURCH STORES
ARE CHEAP CHEAP CHEAP

I was spending a few weeks in New York when the early spring weather suddenly turned unseasonably cold and I hadn't packed any winter clothes. I wandered into a church thrift store that was having a half-price sale on all winter coats. I found a barely used fur-lined raincoat for ten bucks. That puppy kept me toasty warm while the March winds blew. Yes, I sometimes wear fur. There's nothing warmer, and down coats makes you look like a king-size duvet on legs. Besides, I eat very little meat.

FLEA MARKETS

These are fun to browse, but the prices of professional dealers are usually too high for me. If I do go to a flea market, I try to get there for the last hour. That's when the vendors are ready to make deals and clear out the inventory.

By the way, I often see those same vendors picking through the goods at yard sales. And they can sometimes be a little arrogant. Many years ago, I fell in love with Bakelite jewelry and started buying it cheaply on country weekends. I wandered into a fancy-dancy shop off Madison Avenue and saw that they had duplicates of my pieces, so I offered to sell the owner some of my collection. He sneered at me like I was some kind of filthy rag peddler, "Sorry, I do not buy from the street." I held onto my Bakelite, which is worth a lot more now than it was then. Recently, I sold a few pieces to a dealer, who told me that she is a "picker" for that very same shop. I was tempted to include a note: "Regards from the street."

EBAY

This is a tremendous resource for bargainistas. I've gotten everything from Arche sandals to Chantelle bras at lower-than-low prices. It does take a little effort. You have to study the measurements carefully or, better yet, know your size in each label, because all brands vary. High-end European labels tend to run small—yet another reason to hate the French.

CRAIGSLIST

You can find anything on this site, from a one-month sublet to a gently used coffin. Some of the listings are quite poignant, and I often wonder about the back story.

- "Wedding gown, cost over $5,000. Asking $750. Never worn."

- "Huge divorce sale—forty year collection—everything must go."

There's a lot of human drama going on here.

On Craigslist I've also made contact with some trendy new L.A. designers who hold private sales of old samples. Linda Loudermilk had one of her artful organic skirts featured in *The Devil Wears Prada*. I bought a large quantity of clothing (mostly for gifts or resale), so she gave me good prices. One item I kept for myself was a $200 top for which I paid ten bucks. Linda sells to a lot of celebs, so when I wear the top it's the only time I actually have something in common with Paris Hilton.

CONSIGNMENT SHOPS:
SECOND-HAND WITH A FANCY NAME

These profit-making stores sell high-end items in good condition. They don't want to be confused with lower-end thrift stores, and I get a kick out of the various euphemisms: "designer resale," "pre-worn," "gently used," and so on. My favorite is the Australian "pre-loved."

Some of these boutiques can be pricey, but you're still saving a bundle. Catwalk, in Los Angeles, specializes in fine designer fashion, like a Christian Dior floral silk brocade jacket that, two years ago, retailed for $3,500. You can buy it at Catwalk for $900.

A resale shop can be a lifesaver in an emergency. Benni is a friend of the Swedish actor Max von Sydow. One day Max breezed into town and called to invite us to a formal reception to meet his new French wife. I had three days' notice, nothing to wear, and the very limited budget of an unemployed freelance actress/writer.

So I hit Ravishing Resale, my local consignment shop. The glamorous owner, Marouschka, is a friend of mine. (I often consign my yard sale treasures to her.) She had the perfect dress for me: a sexy black beaded cocktail number from Fred Hayman Beverly Hills. I paid $100, which is way above my usual five bucks, but the dress retailed for more than $800, and I didn't have time to shop around.

At the reception, I got to sit with the old Hollywood star Roddy McDowall, who complimented me on my outfit. Max's French bride outdid everyone, though, in a fabulous gown by Moschino. I doubt it was "pre-loved."

SAMPLE SALES

You can find these wherever there is any fashion industry. I search for them on Google or Craigslist. These sales are great if you want brand-new stuff as opposed to pre-worn. I went to one recently and got a $300 Karen Zambos Vintage Couture dress for ten bucks.

RAG HOUSES

These are warehouses for vintage clothing where they sell stuff by weight. A lot of vintage stores and professional eBayers get their inventory here. I go to one, called A & D Wholesale Vintage Clothing, where the price is four bucks a pound. Clearly, this is not the place to buy heavy wool coats, but I picked up a dozen vintage silk Hawaiian shirts for almost nada. Then I brought them on a visit to Denmark, and we took a family photo in cold, gray Copenhagen with everyone in these colorful, tropical shirts. They sure brightened up the gloomy day!

RETAIL ADVENTURES

Once in a great while, I will actually break down and buy something spanking new in a department store, but I wait for deals. I love cashmere; it's the only wool that doesn't give me red, itchy skin. The problem is that pesky little moths love cashmere as much as I do, which means that used items are full of holes. Cashmere is expensive, but Macy's was having a half-price sale, plus I had a coupon for a 20 percent discount. I got a black turtleneck. Original price was $150. I paid sixty bucks.

I didn't do so well when I bought a cashmere robe on eBay. It was brand new, with a Nordstrom's tag of $400. I paid $200, but the sizing was skimpy and it had no pockets. I resold it for $180,

Just when I thought I'd covered every possible outlet for bargainista chic, I saw a little item in *Sunset Magazine* about a store at the Fashion Institute of Design that sells donated new name-brand items for one, two, and five dollars. Can't wait to check it out

There are lots of Web sites for discount fashion shopping. One is Gilt.com, where they sell high-end designer goodies at huge discounts—more than half off. I just saw a listing for a Marc Jacobs black silk gown that retails for $3,200. The Gilt price was $798.

then found a pocketed robe that fit well at Loehmann's for $140. The whole process was an annoying waste of time—not my finest hour.

I sometimes check out the discount chains.

- Ross Dress for Less lives up to its name. I get a lot of my underwear and socks there. A $32 Olga bra sells for $7.50. I also got a $100 Calvin Klein sweater for $25 and some $70 Teva sandals for $20. On Tuesdays, there's a 10 percent discount if you're over fifty-five.

- At Marshalls, I got Benni some eighty-dollar Rockport loafers for thirty bucks.

- A lot of people swear by Target. I saw some soft cotton tees for $3.99, but this store usually doesn't carry labels that inspire me, except when they produce a limited run of low-priced clothing by high-end designers. H & M and The Gap do the same thing, and some of those cheapo designer pieces have become collectors' items.

- Loehmann's is the queen of discount clothing. You can find all the best labels for way less than the original price. I always go there in November for my 15 percent birthday discount, which also coincides with their pre-Christmas sale.

BARGAINISTA SHOPPING ABROAD

When I travel, I shop second-hand just like at home. I've done

- Flea markets in France (a 1920s Deco gold and coral ring).

- Tag sales in Denmark. My brother-in-law, Søren, bought an Armani coat, then came home and discovered money in the pocket—more than he had paid for the coat. Being your typical honest Dane, he returned the money. I don't know if I would have been as noble.

- Thrift shops in England, where I bought nothing. The places smelled of wet wool, and the vast number of large-sized pleated tweed skirts was a turn-off.

When I learned that my son was planning a huge, black-tie wedding, I started planning the most important feature of the event: my dress. I needed an expensive designer gown, but wasn't willing or able to write a fat check for something I would probably never wear again unless they start giving Oscars to bit players. Then I saw in the *L.A. Times* classifieds that the CBS wardrobe department was having a liquidation sale.

I ran over there and spotted the gown of my dreams. It was turquoise silk, with a sparkling beaded bodice, by the prize-winning Carmen Marc Valvo. It fit like a glove—as long as I didn't exhale—and the $1,200 price tag was still dangling. I got it for twenty bucks. The wedding was fabulous, the gown was a big hit, and the price tag is still dangling inside in case I ever want to sell it.

- In New Zealand, the dollar was very strong, so I was able to get a vintage diamond engagement ring at an antique fair for a pittance. This was no impulse buy. At this point, I had been married for thirty years and felt I had waited long enough for a little bling.

$3 Shopping to Stay Fit

Shopping is a great cardiovascular workout. You burn off calories by walking up the escalator, you firm up your upper arms by sliding clothes along the rack, and what's a better weight-bearing exercise than lugging six shearling coats into the dressing room?

When I bend over to try on a pair of lace-up sandals I get a spinal stretch just as effective as the yoga salutation to the sun. As I jiggle in place at the end of the line in the ladies' room I go for the burn of a low-impact aerobics class, and I don't have to put up with the nauseating perkiness of the chirpy instructor.

I can't do my fitness program at Barney's. That's okay. I can throw on some sweats, step into my sneaks, and jog eight long blocks to the local thrift store. An hour later, I speed-walk home, doing arm-lifts with two hefty muscle-building shopping bags. Who says you can't have gain without pain?

$4 A Frugalista's Revenge

A s with any addiction, there came a time when the bargain-shopping pleasure turned to pain. Every closet, shelf, and drawer in the house was overflowing with valuable stuff that was never used. I don't wear the designer clothing because I live in sweatpants. I don't use the crystal salt cellars because I rarely entertain. I don't have the time: I'm much too busy buying crystal salt cellars. After a family intervention, I agreed to go cold turkey. I wouldn't give up treasure hunting, but I would turn my compulsion into a business. I started selling my goodies: some on eBay, some to resale shops, some to private dealers.

It was fun to have a little cottage industry, but like all entrepreneurs, I dreamed of the Big Score: the costume person from a film studio who would be my main buyer. This person would appreciate my exquisite taste and, since they were paying with someone else's dime, would never haggle over the cost. I would sit in the audience and think, "That's my Escada blazer! That's my Weiss necklace!"

And so it came to pass. Twice a year we have a huge yard sale at rock bottom prices to unload the surplus goods. At my last sale, a young woman named Laura S. showed up and announced that she was doing wardrobe for a Dreamworks movie. Just like in my fantasy, Laura gushed over my fabulous taste and phoned her assistant to check the sizes of various actors. She bought Anna Sui and Vivienne Tam and Armani. She bought a Coach bag and some vintage jewelry. She was in a hurry to get back to the set, so I took a check for $400. She promised to come over every month to check out my inventory. My dream had come true: I was in business with Steven Spielberg.

The check bounced. It wasn't just an oversight: The account had been closed for several months. I called Dreamworks and asked for Laura S. No such person. "Are you sure? She's doing wardrobe on *Santa Clause 3*." No, that film was not Dreamworks; it was Disney. I called Disney and learned that the movie had wrapped three months ago. Laura S. was a total fraud. The assistant she talked to was probably a dial tone. Laura played on my greed, my vanity, and my pathetic eagerness to be a professional shopper for the movies.

My miracle had turned into a "be careful what you wish for" fable. It served me right, because as a secular cynic, I ought to know that miracles do not happen—just random events that usually end badly. I was furious, but I was also fascinated by the psychopathology at work here. If you're a skilled con artist, why steal used goods from yard sales? Whatever happened to professional standards? Even criminals should aim high.

I started leaving phone messages for Laura, sometimes several in one day. No reply, of course. We drove to the address on the check. No such person, of course. For many months to come, I was obsessed with revenge fantasies. I thought of all the things I would say and do to Laura S. if I ever ran into her, how I would make a loud scene in public and force her to pay me back.

And so it came to pass. I walked into a lingerie shop not far from home, and there, writing out a check on the same phony checkbook, was Laura S. Just as I had imagined, I yelled to the owner, "Don't take that check! She's a con artist!" Laura looked up and said, just as sweet as could be, "Oh, I'm so glad I found you! I've been looking all over for you! I owe you money!" Yeah, right.

My fantasy script called for me to escort her to a nearby ATM, which I did. As she handed me the cash, she said, "I know you don't believe me, but I'm really not a bad person." "Laura, everything you told me was a lie." "No, I'm exactly what I said. I'm a studio executive." Poor dear. If she had only put her mind to it, she probably could have been. She had all the qualifications.

Labels: I Don't Promote Them, and I Don't Believe Them

Every primitive tribe has its status symbols. Who owns the most goats? Who wears the most beads? Who has the largest lip plate? In the supposedly advanced culture we inhabit, people strut around proudly displaying their labels. Maybe we're not as advanced as we think we are; beads make more sense to me.

I'm not saying there's anything wrong with wanting stuff that's well designed and of good quality. I just don't understood people who buy clothing that broadcasts the maker. Why wear a bag with a pattern that screams, "FendiFendiFendiFendi," unless Fendi is paying you for the free commercial?

Flaunting the brand has no aesthetic value. It doesn't make the item prettier or more flattering; it just shows you can afford to buy something expensive. Well, if that's your goal, why not wear that Marc Jacobs jacket inside out so people can see who made it? Or, better yet, just enlarge the price tag, laminate it, and pin it to the collar?

Anyway, there are so many counterfeits around that the gal with the Vuitton tote ("LVLVLVLVLV") probably got it for a pittance from a street vendor, so you'd better carry around some documentation proving that yours is real.

For years, one of my favorite outfits was a '40s vintage rayon skirt with a sort-of-matching wraparound top. They had two different floral patterns, but the colors were similar enough to relate. Some heavily labeled fashionista ("CoachCoachCoach") came up to me at a dinner party and said, "Lovely ensemble. Missoni?" "Uh, no; thrift shop." The conversation stopped there.

Flash is a performance artist who, like me, loves Sportsac bags. They weigh nothing, they have a million compartments, and they're washable. The only problem is that the LeSportsac name is prominently featured in more than one spot on the exterior. Flash, also like me, is label-allergic, so she took some strips of velvet ribbon and sewed them over the offending display. I admire her creativity, but I confess I'm not enough of a purist to make that much effort. If I have to choose between principles and laziness, laziness will usually win out.

Everyone's jumping on the bargainista bandwagon, but some of the efforts are pretty lame. The *Los Angeles Times* compared a $14.99 Gap T-shirt to a similar Jil Sander number priced at a whopping $205. That price is outrageous! I would *never* spend $14.99 on a T-shirt.

DISREGARD THESE INSTRUCTIONS

I pay no attention to those worthless care labels inside every garment. "Dry Clean Only" is a big fat lie. What did people do before they had chemical dry cleaners? They washed everything. And that's what I do: silk, rayon, linen, everything. I just throw it in the machine, do a cold water wash, and hang it up to dry.

Of course, I've had my disasters. I mistakenly put a DKNY velour turtleneck into a hot water wash and ended up with a top that would fit a Barbie doll. I did something similar with Benni's favorite Brooks Brothers linen shirt, but keep in mind that anything I ruin didn't cost much, so I can afford the occasional mess-up.

Another instruction label I totally disregard is "Hand Wash Only." My philosophy is "Hand Wash Never." I just put flimsy delicates in the gentle cycle, and my manicure will last a few days longer.

$6 Bargaining: Dos and Don'ts

I buy so much stuff that I'm forced to have a ginormous yard sale twice a year, with hundreds of tasty items. It's a great opportunity to study people's bargaining skills. Here are some approaches I do not recommend.

- "How much? That's ridiculous. I could get it cheaper at Kmart."

- "Thirty dollars? I'll give you five."

- "I can't pay ten dollars. Here's one-fifty, but my money is special. It'll bring you good luck."

- "Twenty dollars? Oh gee, I only have eight bucks with me. Will that do?"

  Here are some offers that actually work.

- "You have such cool stuff. If I buy a lot, can you give me something off?"

- "That's a fair price, but it's a little high for me. Any chance you could do better?"

- "I love your hair!"

  That last one gets me every time.

25

It helps to give the seller some insight into who you are. I happen to have a soft spot for teachers. They are undervalued and underpaid for the important work they do. A pleasant young woman at my sale said, "How much for the big box of construction paper and charcoals? I teach special needs kids, and they love craft projects." I gave it to her for free, and she's become one of my regular customers. She always buys clothing for herself, and I pick up paper and art supplies throughout the year to donate to her class.

WHAT CAN YOU LOSE BY ASKING?

You'd be surprised at how many store owners are open to friendly haggling. For starters, you can always ask for a discount if you're paying cash or if you're buying multiple items. My brother-in-law Søren is a champion negotiator who gets markdowns in clothing boutiques, furniture and appliance stores, even hotels. He does this by being charming, sincere, and civil and by believing that it never hurts to ask. Use your judgment, though: All the charisma in the world isn't going to lower the price at the gas pump.

Some people are born without the haggling gene. It's a serious handicap. Kim, one of my best friends, actually said to a flea market vendor, "Only ten dollars for that vase? Oh, no, I feel I should give you twenty." Kim is no longer allowed to come shopping with me, but she's very welcome as a customer at my own sales.

$7 Giveaways

I do love a low price, and you can't get lower than zero. The good news is that there are a gazillion cool items out there that are just yours for the taking—everything from moving boxes to mature trees. (And we all know how irritating immature trees can be.)

The enlightened folks who donate these freebies realize that it makes more sense to give something away than to dump it in the landfill. So when you take someone's electric juicer, you are not just being thrifty; you are protecting the environment. Frugaholics tend to think green.

CRAIGSLIST

This is a great source of freebies of all kinds.

- "Barbie doll house, made of wood, hundreds of small toys inside, with Barbies. Adding a little bike also."

- "One green round plastic patio table w/4 chairs."

- "Free paint cans: black, light yellow, Aztek orange, light green, deep maroon/red."

Occasionally, the offerings get a little bizarre.

"I HAVE THE FOLLOWING ITEMS IN SIZE MEDIUM
5 THONGS (WHITE, RED, BLACK, PINK, PURPLE)
10 HALF SLIPS (2 WHITE, BEIGE, PINK, PURPLE,
BABY BLUE, 2 BLACK, RED, DARK BLUE)
8 BRAS (SAME COLOR AS SLIPS)
3 GARTER BELTS (BLACK, WHITE, RED)
1 CORSET IN WHITE."

Or, on a different note,

"HORSE MANURE YOU HAUL ANY AMOUNT."

I check these listings regularly, because you never know when I might need some horse manure—or a white corset.

In Los Angeles, people often leave unwanted goods at the side of the road. I am still enjoying two patio lounge chairs that I found that way. Over the years, we have picked up all kinds of useful items, including a box of picture frames and a dozen bamboo plants. But I kept on driving past an overstuffed sofa because bedbugs are one of my many phobias—along with crowded elevators and foggy plane landings.

LOCAL PUBLICATIONS

Most cities have periodicals that take free ads for goods being sold or given away. In Los Angeles, we have *The PennySaver* and *The Recycler*. I use them all the time, for both selling and buying.

GIGOIT

This is a terrific Web site with a difficult name where people list things they want to get rid of. You just enter your zip code, see what's being given away in your area, and start hauling.

- "Ex-wife's Mikasa dishes: White with a grey and black edge pattern—service for 8; the whole set is yours for the asking."

- "Litter box trained bunny: It runs around the house like (with) your cat and uses a litter box. Comes with hay, feed and cord protectors to a loving home. She is friendly, fixed and healthy."

- "39 unused Australia/New Zealand postcards: Unused postcards, good for an art project or to send notes."

I find the first two items very tempting. I don't need dishes or a house-trained bunny, but what great deals! Not sure about the last one. Do I really want to drive 5 miles for thirty-nine Australia/New Zealand postcards?

ONLINE COUPONS

There are lots of commercial sites where you can sign on for product coupons or free samples. One such site is www.afullcup.com. I don't do this because I'm afraid of getting on some list that will send me hundreds of daily messages from Procter and Gamble, which seems a high price to pay for a free packet of shampoo.

Here's a mysterious fact: For some reason, there are always perfectly good paper clips lying on the sidewalk. Unless you're germ-phobic—which is one of the few fears I do not have—you can pick up all manner of paper clips, any day of the week. And Mother Earth will smile upon you when those paper clips end up on your desk rather than in the ocean, which is where all street litter ends up.

VIVA LAS VEGAS

If you stay at a hotel in Sin City, chances are you'll subsequently get some terrific offers. I'm not talking about those high rollers who get everything comped. I'm just talking about your garden variety buffet-eating, craps-playing tourist. Last year, for our anniversary, our son, Jonathan, treated us for a weekend at the Wynn. He joined us and paid all expenses for two rooms. Six months later, the hotel offered him three free nights plus $150 in chips. He took the offer and won $1,200 in a poker tournament.

THRIFTY, NOT SHIFTY

There are some cheapies who have no scruples. I know one woman who convinced the owner of a local restaurant that she was a food critic in order to finagle a free dinner.

And then I met someone who bragged that she persuaded the Tourist Board of India that she was doing research for a travel documentary. The government agreed to pay for her ticket and first-class accommodations.

These people are lying, scuzzy thieves who give a bad name to honest cheapazoids like me.

WATCH AND LEARN

Instructional Web sites like Expert Village offer a variety of no-cost mini-classes on any subject imaginable.

• How to Wax Your Pottery Before Glazing

• Playing E Minor 7 in 3rd Inversion Arpeggios on Guitar

• Ending Off a Spiral Knot Hemp Bracelet

I don't know what a spiral knot hemp bracelet is, but if I were making one I would certainly want to know how to end it off. This site is a godsend for people like me, who never leave the house. I just practiced the basic salsa step, and I'm about to learn how to introduce myself in Japanese.

A more cerebral free learning center is TED, which stands for Technology, Entertainment, Design. This highbrow site offers fifteen-minute talks on weighty subjects by the world's great thinkers, plus entertaining pieces by offbeat performance artists. You can watch Stewart Brand, you can watch Jane Goodall, you can watch Bill Clinton. Me, I watched some very funny jugglers.

FREE LOVE

People pay big bucks to join dating services, but there are no-cost ways to make connections. You might start with friends. I was fixed up with Benni on a blind date. We met in February and got married in April, because he had just arrived from Copenhagen and needed a green card. My friends warned me that after he got his papers I might never see him again, but I felt we were a good fit and decided to risk it. That was forty-five years ago, and we're still going strong—except for the constant bickering.

I know one woman who started attending AA meetings in Beverly Hills. She had no addiction problems, but she figured there might be some interesting single men there. I'm not sure I'd recommend that ploy, but there are plenty of classes, church groups, and political and charitable organizations where you can meet people who are not battling substance abuse.

I've been in a few shows directed by my friend Michael. He volunteered to be a mentor to a disadvantaged kid. At the training session, he met a young woman who was also being trained. They have been married for twenty years.

My son, Jonathan, has a friend who joined the Peace Corps. While he was working in Haiti, he hooked up with another volunteer, and the wedding took place a year later.

I'm not saying you have to join a do-good organization to meet your soulmate. I just think that if you have a lot of hobbies, interests, and passions, you just might come across Mr. or Ms. Right in the middle of your active life, without paying a fee.

If I were single in a big city, I'd get a puppy—and not just for companionship. Dog owners are a very social subculture. I took a stroll with my friend Sue and her Wheaton terrier, Daisy, in Manhattan's Riverside Park. We couldn't walk for two minutes without another canine owner stopping to chitchat. Maybe someone should start a business leasing dogs to singles. Call it PuppyPimp.com. I see a film script here.

# $8 Recycling

I am allergic to waste. I just can't abide the thought of perfectly usable things being dumped into the garbage. Besides the ecological consequences, there's the offense to my compulsively thrifty nature. If there's such a thing as reincarnation (which I strongly doubt) I must have been a squirrel. I totally understand the urge to dig a little hole and drop an acorn in, ensuring a tasty snack on a winter day.

THE OLD FOOD MOVEMENT

I love leftovers. When you heat up food the next day, the flavorful juices have been absorbed, and you have a ready-made dinner that doesn't require any work (a big plus in my book). Some cultures have no concept of leftovers; they demand food that's freshly bought and freshly made. Masaki, a film producer from Tokyo, came over and watched me place a pot of yesterday's beef stew on the stove. He couldn't contain his horror. "Annie-san! Are you serving garbage?"

I also know some Americans who won't eat yesterday's food. When I go to their homes for dinner, I bring my own plastic containers so that I don't have to suffer the sight of that yummy lasagna being scraped into the trash. By the way, those plastic containers were not bought in a store. I just save takeout containers; no Tupperware parties for me.

ON THE ROAD

I haven't bought soap, shampoo, conditioner, body lotion, mouthwash, or ballpoint pens in years. That's what hotels are for. I'll admit I sometimes overdo it. We were about to leave for the long trip home from Sydney, Australia. Benni was in the shower and asked for the soap. "Too late. It's already packed!" He did not appreciate my suggestion of just splashing on some extra cologne.

I always travel with those tiny plastic containers of jams and honey that they give you in coffee shops. I learned my lesson the hard way. We were having a croissant and coffee one morning in Paris, and I asked for some jam. They brought a pot of orange marmalade and charged us five euros, which is about eight dollars. Never again.

I also carry those herbal tea packets you get in hotel rooms. I'm allergic to caffeine, and in many places in the world, "decaf" is considered the equivalent of "boorish American" and is not available. Even domestic airlines can be a problem. I was traveling first class on United and got a packet of decaffeinated coffee and a cup of lukewarm water that wasn't hot enough to dissolve the coarse powder. So I couldn't drink my coffee; I had to chew it.

A FEW TIPS—
MOSTLY SENSIBLE, SOME A LITTLE WEIRD

- I never buy garbage bags. When they ask "Plastic or paper?" in the supermarket, I just take the plastic and then use them for trash. This has gotten problematic because I'm trying to reduce my big fat carbon footprint. I now bring reusable canvas shopping bags to the store, but where am I supposed to put my garbage? A friend bought biodegradable trash bags. They worked so well that they biodegraded while still in the kitchen bin.

- I never buy wrapping paper. I've endured too many Christmas celebrations, wedding showers, and birthday parties that ended with a mountain of gift-wrap trash. Some Martha Stewart types save it all for craft projects, but I'd rather have a colonoscopy than do a craft project. Instead, I put presents into those gift bags that are two for a dollar at the Ninety-Nine Cent Store. I don't write on the message tag, so the recipient can use the bag again. Anyway, if I try to wrap a package myself, it comes out looking like the work of a four-year-old, so the bags save me a lot of stress.

- I do not throw out old clothing. I donate it to my local thrift shop. This sometimes ends badly, when I mistakenly buy my own stuff back.

- I reuse shoe boxes as storage containers. I suspect I was not the first to think of this one.

- I buy a bag of 100 clothespins at the Ninety-Nine Cent Store and use them to close half-used bags of chips. A package of three plastic chip-clips in the supermarket would be four bucks.

- I use the free address labels that come in the mail as IDs on cell phones, manuscripts, and so on. (I was going to put one on my key chain, then thought better of it.)

- I received some gift bouquets that came in lovely ceramic containers. I already own around twenty-five lovely ceramic containers, so I saved the ones from the florist and sold them at my yard sale.

- I take the pile of extra paper napkins from the pizza place and keep them in the car.

- I use free supermarket plastic produce bags instead of buying plastic wrap.

- I rinse off and reuse aluminum foil.

- I put the clean side of paper back into the printer for double duty. (Do not do this if you're sending in a job application.)

- When I'm finished with a magazine, I give it to my local manicure salon.

- And here's a real shocker: I occasionally flip my underwear to save on washing machine use. On those days, I pray that I won't be visiting the emergency room.

- One group in Boston, Extras for Creative Learning, collects surplus office supplies from businesses and then distributes them to undersupplied schools.

- Shhhh Salvage gets tons of about-to-be-trashed fabric from Broadway plays, fashion shows, weddings, and so on, then sells them cheaply to other productions. This is the kind of profit-making enterprise I call "doing well by doing good."

House Beautiful

PART

II

$1 Renting Versus Owning

T he common wisdom is that it makes more sense to buy rather than rent. Real estate goes up in value, they say (whoever *they* are), and you get a tax break on the mortgage interest. But common wisdom has its flaws. True, I know people who bought Manhattan co-ops in the '80s for pocket change and then made millions. I also know folks who now have to move in with their married kids after losing their homes.

WOULDA, COULDA, SHOULDA

We used to own an apartment on Manhattan's Upper West Side and a weekend house in Columbia County, about two hours north of the city. We sold them both after moving to Los Angeles. Since that time, both areas have become popular, trendy, and costly.

The six-room apartment we sold for $400,000 in 1992 sold in 2007 for $1.8 million. The cottage on a hill near Hudson, New York, brought us $60,000 and is now worth more than $200,000. Ouch!

Because we paid very little, we did make some money on each sale, but not the killing we would have made if we had held on longer and sold during the boom. When I have attacks of self-pity, Benni gives me a dose of reality. He points out that we would have struggled for fifteen years to come up with increased maintenance fees, higher real estate taxes, and constant repairs. Having a low rent during those years allowed us extra money for important things like theater tickets and restaurants. Twelve years of eating at home every night is not worth any price.

A LEASE ON LIFE

I'm much happier as a renter. First of all, I hate responsibility. Owning a house can be a chain around your neck, and I want a lifestyle that's as flexible and stress-free as possible. If a polka band moves in next door, I need to be able to move on a moment's notice.

Also, houses are money pits. There's always some nasty problem: sewage issues, leaky roofs, termites, whatever. I don't want to have to replace a furnace or fix the plumbing or hire a crew to prune the dead treetops. I just call my landlord. Some people do a lot of this stuff themselves, but Benni takes three weeks to change a lightbulb, and he's the handy one in the family.

Lots of people want reliable house-sitters when they leave town, especially if they have pets. My actress friend Mariann had to spend some time in L.A. and was trying to live on the cheap. An acquaintance was leaving her L.A. condo to work in London for eight months. Mariann got the condo and the car in return for babysitting two cats.

You might consider hiring on as a building manager. You get an apartment in return for maintaining the premises and collecting rent. It's usually not more than a part-time job, and you're paying zero rent.

LET IT ALL OUT

Whether we owned or rented, we always made money by subletting if we were going to be away for a while. We don't do it any more because Benni has amassed a collection of 10,000 rare books that can't be touched, moved, or looked at.

I had certain standards about finding the right tenant: no shares and no lawyers. I didn't want three surfer dudes trashing the place with crushed brewski cans, and lawyers tend to be—guess what?—litigious. One guy called and said he was an attorney, and I made some lame excuse to get rid of him.

"I know what's going on here. You don't want me as a tenant because I'm a lawyer. I could sue you for that!" I rest my case.

Even with all my precautions, we sometimes had problems.

- At one interview, a young woman asked how often she should shampoo the sofa. Since I didn't even know that sofas could *be* shampooed, I figured she was a good bet. One month into her stay, she stopped paying rent. We were in Japan at the time, so evicting her was no easy task. After that experience, I always demanded full payment in advance.

- Another tenant called us in Denmark to complain that the light-bulb in the kitchen had burned out.

- Someone else decided to get creative and rearranged all the furniture. He moved a fragile antique lamp from the living room onto a narrow counter in the bathroom. The lamp survived, but I did not appreciate the extreme makeover.

These were the exceptions. Most of our tenants were pleasant and responsible, and we even formed friendships with a few of them. The important thing was that we covered our rent—and then some—while we were away. Our oddest subletter was a rich Beverly Hills lady who was getting a divorce. Just after we left town, she reconciled with her husband. She never moved in and never asked us to return the two months' rent: the dream tenant!

Here are some other people who use their homes for income.

- Rowena helps me develop the voices for my solo shows. She goes to Australia a few times a year to teach vocal technique to actors. She takes out an ad on Craigslist and never has trouble finding a short-term tenant for her L.A. condo.

- Mary is the mother of one of Jonathan's college buddies. When her husband died, her large townhouse was a lonely space. She decided to rent a room to a college student, which gives her income and occasional companionship.

- Jonathan's colleague Guy owns a small apartment in Paris; my friend Julie has a country house in the south of France. They each do very well with short-term rentals. Of course, these are attractive locations. You won't earn too much renting your condo in Chernobyl.

$2 The Weekend House

A lot of city people dream of having a country place where they can chill out from the pressures of urban life and stop and smell the roses. We had such a place in upstate New York. Believe me, there was no time for rose smelling. There was rose planting, rose pruning, and rose feeding. Then there was cleaning, shopping, entertaining, laundering, cooking, and commuting. Sunday nights back in Manhattan I would not be refreshed and renewed: I'd be totally exhausted, wondering where the weekend went.

If you are brave (or foolish) enough to commit to the labor of a country place, be sure you and the real estate agent are on the same page. I told the broker we wanted an older home with a view. He took us to a ranch house facing the highway. I should have known then that there might be some cultural clashes between me and the local people—like the time I unfolded a patchwork quilt at a yard sale and pointed out a large hole to the owner. She said, "I hate when you city people come here and try to Jew me down!" So much for "small town values."

Every Friday night we loaded up the car with

- Two cats who disappeared every Sunday when it was time to head back to the city. It usually took an hour searching in the poison ivy–filled woods to find them.

- A sulky kid who hated the country and would only come if he could bring along a sulky friend.

- A huge assortment of urban necessities that we couldn't get up in the sticks, like fresh pasta.

- And—because I'm a lunatic—a container of food scraps I had saved all week to add to the mulch pile. Yes, even garbage has value to a committed thriftaholic.

When we started spending more time in Los Angeles, I got calls from our country neighbors with messages like, "There was a big storm last night and one of your trees crashed into your roof." And I had to deal with this from 3,000 miles away. Not a good formula for a stress-free life.

After we sold the house, I realized that you don't have to own a garden to enjoy one. That's what resorts are for. And parks. And botanical gardens. And friends with weekend houses. When I'm a guest, I have plenty of time to smell the roses. And I'm not the one writing the check when a tree crashes into the roof.

The whole country house debacle just confirmed my suspicions that

LIVING SIMPLY = LIVING CHEAPLY = LIVING HAPPILY

I think I'll put that on a T-shirt.

George and Alice are old college friends who live in the Berkshires. Years ago they bought a small beachfront property on Nantucket for a second home. They asked the dean of architecture at Yale to recommend a young but promising designer. The house got built for $80,000, and summer rentals were a good source of income. Several years ago, George and Alice decided to sell the house and use the money to travel to exotic places. The young but promising designer had meanwhile morphed into notable architect Robert Venturi. The little beachfront house was considered an architectural gem, and it sold for more than $2 million.

Interior Design

We all want a comfortable home filled with beautiful things, but there are different ways of getting there. I want only furnishings that will increase in value, which leaves out Ikea, Pottery Barn, department stores, and other (shudder) retail establishments.

FLOOR COVERINGS

Wall-to-wall carpeting is not for me. Not only is it bland and allergen filled, but you can't buy it second-hand. Anyway, I much prefer the rich warmth of antique rugs on wooden floors, but they have to be real. I don't know why anyone would throw away good money on a machine-made, mass-produced "Oriental rug" when you can get the genuine hand-loomed article at an estate sale or auction for a trifle. I have a collection of Chinese Deco rugs from the '20s (one is one the cover), and I don't think I paid more than one or two hundred dollars for any of them. They are worth a lot more. I will admit that they are not all in perfect condition, but life is compromise.

Some folks spend a fortune on marble or ceramic tile floors. They can be beautiful, but they're also cold under bare feet. Plus they're slippery and so hard that you could split your head open if you fall. There are cheaper options. An artist friend splatter-painted the cement floor of her studio. It looks great, and I'd love to do that in my kitchen, but I'm not sure my landlord will go for it. He's more of a monochrome beige kind of guy. He did, however, allow me to replace a worn-out bathroom floor with inexpensive black and white vinyl tiles from Home Depot. They complement the 1920s Mediterranean style of the house. Not quite as authentic as ceramic tiles but good enough for me.

In fact, I've always liked linoleum, which has been out of fashion since the '50s. Now, they say it's coming back. This is no surprise, because interior design trends are cyclical. By the time every little studio apartment has granite countertops, you can be pretty sure that granite countertops will be on the way out, and Formica will be on the way in.

OLDIES BUT GOODIES

I started collecting antiques when we had a country house. The main form of entertainment on Saturday night was the local auction. I bid on everything from a burgundy velvet Victorian armchair ($20) to an old leaded glass lamp ($17) to a cherry music cabinet ($15). Of course, this took place a zillion years ago, and prices are a little higher now, but there are still many treasures to be found. I just scored a 1930s oak dresser with the original hardware for thirty bucks.

NEWBIES BUT GOODIES

If your taste runs more to modernism, there are plenty of gems to be had very cheaply. In my resale wanderings, I've seen everything from Eames tables to Heller dishes to Marimekko fabrics. If you're a serious modernist maven who collects a specific designer, don't forget Craigslist. I just saw an ad for an authentic midcentury coffee table with two tulip chairs by Eero Saarinen priced at a measly $250. You can check eBay as well for fine authentic pieces.

NO GOODIES AT ALL

Suppose you have to furnish a dorm room for a college kid. I would not recommend new. I would not recommend vintage. I would recommend plain old ordinary used. Everything is just going to get scratched, dented, and stained within a month, so why waste money on good stuff? Run-of-the-mill computer desks are one of the most common resale items, as are bookshelves and desk lamps. The money you save could be used for a surgically inserted tracking device so that you know where your Joe College is at all times.

FREE LOOT

My good friend Mimi is a pet portrait painter. Like me, she grew up in the Bronx and married a Dane. Like me, she is a committed frugalista. Her home in Greenwich Village is full of quirky, beautiful, valuable objects and fine old furniture, much of which she has scavenged. When she first started decorating, she found out that the sanitation department picks up large items on Saturdays. So every Friday night, she and her husband scoured the fancier neighborhoods in a truck and brought home high-quality furniture that was being trashed.

One of Mimi's prizes was a nineteenth-century loveseat with an intricately carved frame. Recently, she decided to replace it with something more comfortable. There was a brand new $3,000 sofa in her local thrift store, and the asking price was $895. She waited until it went down to $400, then brought it home and sold the scavenged loveseat for $300.

The house next door was being renovated, and the workers kept throwing stuff into a dumpster. Mimi found a large, intact glass door for her balcony and an old mahogany mantelpiece for the dining room. Dumpster shopping is not for the faint hearted, but it can really pay off, plus you're reducing waste. Mimi's husband is a carpenter and builder, so that helps. My husband is neither a carpenter nor a builder, so I won't be diving for mantelpieces anytime soon.

TRANSFORMATIONS

When we got married, we went to Copenhagen to visit Benni's family and made our first furniture purchase: four bentwood chairs to be shipped to New York. (This was in the good old days when the dollar was strong, shipping was cheap, and Europe was an American shopper's romper room.)

Back in Manhattan we waited, and waited, and waited. The chairs never arrived. The store finally confessed that the shipment had been lost, and they sent over a replacement set. A month later, the original chairs finally showed up. I did not offer to ship them back. I figured I was owed something for three months of eating on the floor.

Many years later, the eight chairs were still sturdy, but they badly needed a facelift. Benni painted them with various multicolor designs, some geometric, some floral. They went from being an ordinary bunch of scruffy old chairs to eye-popping works of art. Everyone admires them and, even though I love them, I can't help wondering how much I could get for them. (One is on the cover of this book. Make me an offer!)

WINDOW MISTREATMENTS

I was a guest at an embassy dinner in New York, and the wife of the Norwegian consul general described the ups and downs of her nomadic life. "We settle into a foreign country, and Lars usually get transferred just when I've finally completed sewing all the curtains for our residence." That's typically Scandinavian. Even prosperous women in the Nordic countries sit and sew their own curtains.

If that works for you, fine; you'll save a bundle. Personally, I'd rather have root canal—not only because I have no patience or time or talent for craft projects but because those home-sewn numbers are plain and boring, and I like window coverings with a little style.

My house is adorned with curtains, drapes, and hardware that I found at yard sales. I've rarely paid more than five bucks a pair. When I got tired of the 1950s floral barkcloth panels in my office, I sold them on eBay—at a profit.

Á LA TABLE

I just bought a huge lot of ovenproof stoneware dishes (dinner plates, salad plates, bowls, cups, and saucers) for forty people—yes, forty—for which I paid thirty dollars at a church sale. That comes to about six and a half cents a dish. This purchase alone qualifies me for a gold medal in bargain hunting, which I think should be a new Olympic sport.

I've picked up a lot of glassware over the years, for about fifty cents a piece. My current favorites are a set of hand-blown Mexican wine glasses. The bowls are clear, with irregular bubbles, and each stem is shaped into a beautiful green glass cactus.

If you're lucky, you might acquire valuable goodies by inheritance. My Danish mother-in-law gave me her magnificent set of 1930s silverware because Benni's siblings prefer modern stainless steel. I cherished it for ages, and when our son got married I passed it on to him. I now use the Bakelite flatware that I've been collecting for years. The colors are mismatched, but I think that adds to the charm. Things can still be beautiful even if they're imperfect—or so I keep telling myself when I look in the mirror.

Picture frames, like eyeglass frames, have an incredibly high markup. I don't mean the mass-produced made-in-China numbers you find at Kmart; I'm talking about the frame that has to be custom made to a certain size. We avoid the middleman and go right to the source. In Los Angeles, it's called Valley Frame and Molding. These wholesale places exist all over, and the price is a fraction of what you'd pay at the frame store. You bring your measurements and choose from a staggering variety of styles and materials, which are then cut to order. As with many wholesale places, you don't have to be a pro to shop here; you just have to open an account.

$4 Art and Collectibles

I'm lucky enough to live in Los Angeles, a city that is always in transition. The nouveau riche here change their wardrobes every year, their houses every other year, and their marriages every couple of months. There are year-round moving sales, which have allowed me to build up my collections of signed art glass, California pottery, '40s tablecloths, and other collectibles.

The worst sales I've ever been to were in genteel, prosperous New England—you know, those towns with white picket fences and village greens, where everybody went to Yale and owns at least one horse. Lots of wealth there, and the crappiest goods I've ever seen. That's because old-money Yankees never throw the good stuff out. They just store it until it becomes chic again.

BOOKWORM

Benni was always interested in fine books and had a modest collection. About ten years ago I was performing in Florida, and we wandered into a thrift store to kill time. Benni bought four volumes for a few bucks.

- A biography of Henry Miller

- A history of ancient Rome

- An obscure collection of poetry

- A weird little volume about magic tricks

When we got home, he looked them up on the Internet just out of curiosity and discovered they were worth quite a bit more than he paid. He sold them on eBay for $400 and got inspired to start a little hobby business. He now has 10,000 books in his inventory, which is fun and profitable for him but problematic for me: I no longer have any shelf or wall or garage space and have to store my candlesticks in a sock drawer.

Benni's primary profession is producing low-budget independent films (*Babette's Feast, Forever Plaid*), which means his days are filled with frustration, aggravation, and chronic unemployment. It takes years to develop and—if you're lucky—complete a movie project. And then, more often than not, the results are abysmal, both artistically and financially.

Selling rare books from home, on the other hand, allows my hubby to earn extra income while enjoying pleasant, civilized contact with people from all corners of the world—like the man whose father had been a missionary in Zanzibar and expressed his heartfelt gratitude for the book that contained a photo of his father's African house.

More than 100 million book titles are listed on the Internet. If you want to know what a book is worth, go to Abebooks and Alibris. There's also Barnes & Noble, Borders, and Amazon. The most common mistake in book collecting is the assumption that a volume is valuable if it's a first edition. It ain't necessarily so. Most books are first editions and don't sell enough to warrant subsequent printings. So if you're reading a first edition of my book, I advise you to buy a few thousand copies in order to increase its future value.

Library sales are a great source. I picked up a little volume about a German artist. All the plates were covered with that see-through paper called tissue guard, so I figured it was worth the fifty-cent asking price. Benni sold it for $300 and gave me a title: VP of acquisitions.

When we're hunting for treasures at yard sales, our mantra is "You never know." You can't judge the quality of the goods by the appearance of a house or its inhabitants. We walked into an unkempt home that smelled of cat piss, and a guy in an undershirt was sitting at a coffee table covered with filled ashtrays. I decided to go no further and went out to wait in the car while Benni wasted his time checking out the books. It turned out not to be such a waste. He found an edition of Andy Warhol prints that had Warhol's signature, plus a little drawing. He paid five bucks to the cat piss guy and sold it for $250. If it weren't for the funky odor, he would have gotten twice that.

Another big score was a book about Mexican artist Diego Rivera. There were three loose photographs inside by Tina Modotti, each with her ink stamp on the back. I never heard of her, but apparently somebody did, because they paid $3,000 for the set. The Diego Rivera book had cost fifty cents.

DUMB

These were a few of our great scores, but we're not always so lucky. We've made many idiotic mistakes, like the violin we bought at a country yard sale for thirty bucks because it had a *Stradivarius* label inside. This label was machine-printed on a piece of paper, which should have been a clue that it was a fake.

I humiliated myself by taking it to a renowned violin expert in Carnegie Hall. I guess he pegged me for a moron as soon as I walked in the door because as I was opening the case he said, dripping with irony, "So what have we got here? A Stradivarius?" Before I even got the violin out of the case, he took one look at it, covered his eyes with his hands, and said, "Put it back! Put it back and get it out of here!" Jeez! People should be kinder to ignoramuses. Did I mention he was French?

Not willing to give up on the "Strad," I brought it to the Metropolitan Museum of Art, having heard that you can get free appraisals at museums and auction galleries. The very kind expert (she was not French) told me that my violin was nineteenth-century Italian, but the cost of repairs would not have been worth it. So at least it wasn't a total piece of junk—just worthless.

AND DUMBER

When we first got married, we were friendly with a poor, shy young artist who had just arrived in New York from Nashville. Whenever he came over, he would bring a gift of a poster, an etching, a lithograph, whatever. His name was Red Grooms, and his work is now very highly regarded. I have seven of his pieces hanging in my dining room. The stupid thing is that I lost, misplaced, gave away about five other of Red's gifts. Even worse, Red asked me to pose for him, and I never found the time. My image could be hanging at the Smithsonian. I am too dumb to live!

AN EYE FOR VALUE

Mimi, the pet portraitist, spends her summers in Denmark, scouring the flea markets around Copenhagen. She collects nineteenth-century Danish landscape paintings and gets them very cheaply because she buys pieces that are torn, stained, or damaged in some way and then repairs them herself. She also buys antique Danish pottery. If there's a chip, she refinishes it. Her beach house, which she and her Viking husband built themselves, houses a collection of beautiful old things that she has paid almost nothing for.

She often buys goodies for resale. One day she showed me a huge vase marked "Amphora, Czechoslovakia." We laughed at the baroque hideousness of the ornate, oversized adornments of turtles and frogs. She had picked it up for fifty kroner (around nine bucks) because she suspected it might be worth something. She wrapped it in a sweater, threw it in her suitcase, brought it back to New York, and sold it to a collector of ugliness for $500. That collector got a good deal: I just saw an Amphora vase on Antiques Road Show that was valued at a thousand bucks, but Mimi was perfectly happy with her 5,000 percent profit. Why be greedy?

FOLLOW YOUR HEART

When we lived in New York, our cat, Samson, disappeared, and the doorman told me that Mrs. Schloss, in 2B, had found him. I rang her bell, and when she invited me in, a bizarre sight greeted me. I saw a large apartment with peeling walls and shabby furniture where every possible surface—the floor, the tables, the sofas, the chairs—was covered with clay figurines. This unassuming retired schoolteacher had a spectacular collection of ancient Chinese burial art.

She explained that she and her husband had never earned much money, but they developed a passion for tomb art before anyone else appreciated it. For many years, they scrimped and saved and bought one piece at a time. When her husband became sick, she needed funds for his medical expenses, so she decided to try to sell some of her beloved sculptures. She was shocked to learn that her collection was worth millions. It became world renowned, and folks like Jacqueline Onassis came to view it. After her husband died, Mrs. Schloss showed her art in museums all over the world—and got marriage proposals from men she had never met.

She was a sweet, eccentric woman who never changed her modest schoolmarm lifestyle. She disapproved of spending money on taxis, so I would see her pedaling down Broadway on her bicycle. In the basket, there was often an object wrapped in a sheet. Sometimes I would catch a glimpse of a ceramic hand poking through the covering—a ceramic hand from 200 B.C. worth a few hundred thousand dollars.

How Does My Garden Grow?

Gardening is a low-cost pleasure. There is something meditative about being in nature, making things grow. My cousin Gordon keeps a dwarf lemon tree in his sunny Connecticut dining room. Gordon artificially inseminates the plant by pretending to be a bee: He gently rubs the center of each blossom with a Q-tip. I've seen bright yellow lemons on Gordon's tree on a snowy winter day. To a brown-thumbed dolt like me, this is magic.

I've never understood the mysteries of pruning, trimming, dividing, feeding, thinning, dead-heading, and so on. Benni is just as horticulturally challenged as I am. I ordered some ground cover from a catalogue for our country home. These tiny naked brown hairy things arrived in little plastic bags, and we spent the afternoon digging them into a slope. A neighbor passed by as we were resting our aching backs and asked why all the roots were sticking up in the air. What a dumb question: the answer was obvious. We had spent a laborious afternoon putting fifty plants into the ground upside down.

Things got easier when we moved to L.A., because everything grows here, even for lazy incompetents like me. Our house is a rental, so I haven't invested in serious landscaping. I just have a hodgepodge of vegetation from various inexpensive sources.

FREE AND ALMOST FREE

Some of my plants were cuttings or exchanges from friends. Every gardener has surplus plantings. I myself have given away enough agave to make a case of tequila. I've also been on the receiving end of other people's surplus, like some heirloom tomatoes, L.A.'s trendiest veggie. And since zero is my favorite number, I'm about to follow up on a Craigslist ad for free bromeliads.

Other plants were bought at farmers' markets, where the prices are much lower than at the stores. I just paid seventy-five cents for a six-pack of impatiens, which would have been $2.50 at the nursery.

I'D LIKE TO THANK MY AGENT

My greatest gardening triumph was my Creative Artists Agency geranium. I was walking past the CAA building in Beverly Hills, which was adorned with many bright red geraniums. One 4-inch stem had broken off and was lying on the pavement. I rescued it and stuck it in the ground when I got home. It grew into a thick, healthy shrub.

Then my landlord decided to put up a 6-foot-high chain link fence along one side of the house, creating all the cozy charm of a prison yard. I cut a dozen stems from my CAA shrub and planted them along the noxious fence. Today, what separates us from the house next door is a 6-foot-high wall of thick greenery dotted with sunny red flowers. Cost to me: nada. Plus, I have the added prestige of having the only fence in Los Angeles that is represented by CAA.

SUPERMARKET GARDENING

I was about to eat a pineapple, but first I sliced off the top and stuck it in a pot. It developed into a nice, spiky green plant and after a few years, in spite of being totally neglected, it miraculously grew a fruit. In a pot. Nature is astounding. Now I think I'll try a mango, a papaya, and a peach. Free fruit salad!

H_2O

Water is scarce and costly in Los Angeles, so I do what I can to recycle it. I keep plastic bowls in the kitchen and bathroom sinks and in the shower to trap the precious liquid, which I then transfer to watering cans. I used to hose down my garden twice a week. Since I've started the catch-it-in-a-bowl system, I've been able to eliminate one of the weekly hosings. I also keep a pitcher of leftover coffee, which I feed to acid-loving plants. This beats buying chemicals at the nursery. Your azaleas will thank you for that cup of joe. But don't use coffee grounds: They bring nasty bugs.

Most of my soil is in the shade, so I buy huge pots at yard sales, fill them with tomatoes, basil, and wild strawberries, and place them in a sunny spot near the garage.

LAWN-O-PHOBE

I don't get the American obsession with green, grassy lawns. I've read that it's based on an unconscious nostalgia for British country mansions. Maybe a big grassy plot makes sense if you live in a wet climate and have to throw tea parties for a few hundred dukes and duchesses, but most of us common folk use our lawns only when we're mowing, watering, or fertilizing them.

Across the country, between 30 and 60 percent of water usage goes to watering lawns. I wonder how many kazillion gallons of our precious H_2O that adds up to.

Also, lawns use more pesticide and herbicide per acre than just about any crop grown in America. We pay good money for these poisons, which are then introduced into our water supply. Plus, those gas-powered noise-polluting mowers and trimmers deplete the ozone layer.

Then there's the aesthetic: The grass lawn that used to be a symbol of aristocracy is now the image of ticky-tacky suburban conformity.

So let's see: Grass lawns are costly, toxic, and boring. Not this baby's idea of a bargain. If you can't eat it, smell it, put it in a vase, or smoke it, why bother?

COVER-UPS

If you absolutely have to have a green carpet, clover is a good choice. It's cheaper and less polluting than lawn grass because it doesn't need fertilizing. Also, its flowers attract bees, and bees create an ecosystem. I couldn't really tell you what an ecosystem is, but I know it's a good thing.

There are drought-resistant ground covers for hot, dry areas and low-maintenance ground covers for cooler climates. A lot of these guys have pretty little flowers, and who doesn't love pretty little flowers?

GROUND ZERO

Xeriscaping uses native plants that to do not need any watering and demand very little maintenance. I respect the no-work ecological concept, but I'm not a fan of that arid desert look. At least, that's what I thought until I saw some xeriscapes that were amazingly green and lush.

I met a woman in Seattle who has an edible garden in front of her house featuring a variety of fruit trees, herbs, strawberries, and vegetables. It's full of color and full of life. However, some unenlightened communities find front yard veggies objectionable. This is another archaic upper-class English tradition: Edibles must always be planted out of sight. I guess the Brits consider food to be terribly vulgar. Well, what do you expect from a country whose national dish is beans on toast?

Christmas lights are among the most common yard sale items. I bought them very cheaply, then waited for a visit from my Danish brother-in-law, Søren, who teaches theatrical lighting design. He strung the lights through all the trees in my little backyard, and the twinkly effect is so enchanting that I might actually consider inviting someone over for an alfresco dinner.

BRICK BY BRICK

People are always giving away building and landscaping supplies. If you don't have friends who are remodeling, there are many ads for freebies on Craigslist. Our pals Tony and Kim had just finished a building project, and they offered us a ton of bricks (!), which we used as garden edging. It was a lot classier than the hideous brown rubbery plastic stuff that I had wasted good money on at Home Depot. Shame on me!

I give high marks to a not-quite-legal movement called guerrilla gardening. These urban activists find a weedy, dirty, unused plot of landscape and drop seed bombs on it, turning it into a city garden. What a cool idea! Make shrubs, not war.

Modern Conveniences—Sometimes

Most appliances do only half the job—like my dishwasher, which washes only clean dishes. I should confess that I do not own top-of-the-line equipment: partly because it's too expensive and partly because I prefer a homey, old-fashioned, shabby-chic look. I have a moneyed friend whose state-of-the-art floor-to-ceiling stainless steel kitchen has all the warmth of a morgue from one of those TV crime shows. Whenever she pulls out a refrigerator bin, I half expect to see a mutilated corpse. "That rib roast was really butchered. Any signs of sexual assault?"

Maybe my dishwasher would do a better job if I used it immediately after dinner, but I do only one load a week. I might eat some cherry pie on Tuesday and not do a wash until Saturday. Unless I thoroughly rinse the plate first, I will have sticky cherry guck etched into that plate forever.

Rinsing your dinner dishes under running water can use up to 25 gallons. I keep a bowl in the sink and rinse everything in the same small amount of water. Then, as I mentioned before, I take that water and pour it into my garden. The pansies don't seem to mind a little cherry juice.

SECOND-HAND SORROWS

I buy most of my household equipment at moving sales, and I've had pretty good luck—except for the time I bought an Amana refrigerator. I went home to have the used appliance store haul the old fridge away. Then we went back to pick up the new one, and I couldn't remember the address of the sale. So we had no refrigerator at all. We drove around Santa Monica for two hours until we finally came to the right street. By the time we got home, all my frozen food had melted in the kitchen sink.

At another sale, we bought a brand new washer and dryer for $200, brought them home, and realized that the new units were electric, not gas, which we had been using. We then had to hire an electrician to install new wiring.

I also forgot to take the instruction manual, so I still don't know what the dial marked "Finish Guard" means. No matter; I don't seem to need it. Anyway, instruction manuals aren't all that useful. I once bought a hair dryer with a directive that warned "Caution: Do Not Use While Sleeping."

ASSAULT AND BATTERY

My favorite modern gizmo is a little foamer that whips up milk for my decaf cinnamon latte every morning. I started feeling guilty about how often I replaced the batteries—not just about the cost but about the impact on the environment. (Guilt is a driving force in my frugalism.) Alkaline batteries cannot be recycled: poison forever.

Benni had just purchased a new digital camera that came with a recharger, so I decided to invest in some rechargeable double-As. A pack of four at the store costs twenty dollars. I got it for five bucks on eBay. These batteries can be recharged a thousand times. That's a lotta latte.

STEAMING MAD

I also like my Jiffy steamer, which I found on Craigslist for twenty-five bucks. It is much better and easier than ironing for silks, linens, and knits. It's also handy for last-minute de-creasing of Benni's suits and blazers, which always need sprucing up. Benni is a shameless clothing abuser, and these suits and blazers are thrown haphazardly onto wire hangers and shoved into a jam-packed closet. Where is Joan Crawford when you need her?

DRY WIT

I still use an old-fashioned rack for smaller items instead of blasting the electric dryer. It saves energy and money, and the rack-dried lingerie has a pleasant, fresh scent. Some activists have gone even further and started a line-drying movement. That could be problematic for city dwellers, although my son lived in a London apartment that had a drying rack that one pulled down from the ceiling, which I thought was a jolly good idea.

Whenever you buy the latest thing in electronics, you can be sure that it'll be smaller, faster, and cheaper six months later. I pity all those suckers who slept in the street the night before the first iPhones hit the stores. A better, less expensive version hit the market within the year.

CALL ME

A lot of people I know are giving up their land lines and just using their cells, to save money. I'm all for saving money, but the reception in many homes sucks, and I am not willing to walk out the door and halfway down the block every time the phone rings. Also, corded phones are more reliable in blackouts, so here, in earthquake-land, fear wins the day.

Skype is a free download, and it's a great way to call long distance. We put a twenty-six-dollar Webcam on my computer, and our Danish family did the same. We can now call Copenhagen, see how the kids are growing, and speak for hours at no cost. The only fly in this ointment is that now I feel obliged to get dressed and made-up before phoning.

THE GOOD OLD DAYS

I'm no Luddite, but I must admit I am nostalgic for some handy and inexpensive bygone technology.

- It was so easy to record from TV with a VCR. That's how I acquired most of my exercise tapes.

- Ceiling fans create a pleasant, cooling breeze that no artificial air conditioner can match. Of course, these still exist, but a well-designed one is hard to find at yard sales.

- Audiocassette players will soon go the way of the typewriter, but I'm holding on to mine. I used to record all my singing lessons and still use those tapes as warm-ups when I perform.

- Lawn blowers make no sense. The noise is deafening (literally), they spray dust over garden furniture and windows, and the fumes pollute the atmosphere. The job they do could easily be performed by a pair of hands and a rake.

Benni's Danish business associate, Erik, had an elderly uncle who needed a new TV. Since the man was ninety-four, Eric figured it would be cheaper to lease a set for the year or so his uncle had left. (TVs are very costly in Denmark.) The uncle spitefully hung on until he was 103, and Erik could have bought many TV sets for the price of the lease.

 **Utilities**

My darling Benni is a utility hog. He leaves the lights on in the bathroom, the TV on in the living room, and the gas on under the coffeepot. Since we both work at home, this means that I spend my day turning off, switching off, and clicking off. I've asked hubby many times why he wants to waste energy and money this way, and his lucid explanation is, "Leave me alone."

I read somewhere that the single most important thing we can do to slow global warming is to reduce our electricity use. When the earth explodes in a ball of fire, I will at least have the satisfaction of blaming my husband.

DIRTY LITTLE SECRETS

I try to save money and conserve precious resources. For example, I do not shower every day. (I don't really need to: I spend most of my time sitting on my butt at the computer, so I rarely work up much of a sweat.) On no-shower days, I wash the essentials at the sink, and with a little deodorant and perfume I'm good to go. On the other hand, I know a woman who takes a shower every morning and a bath at bedtime. That's a little too clean for me, and much too wasteful. Also, water dries your skin, so the shower and bath woman must use lotion by the gallon.

Here's a shocker: I also don't flush every time. It's really not necessary; just put the lid down. However, this custom can be embarrassing if an unexpected guest drops by and wants to use the facilities.

71

My friend Tony put in solar power when he built his house, and he installed something called a pedal valve at his kitchen sink. He presses on a pump with his foot so that the water runs only when he needs it. These greeny things are expensive at first, but the savings accumulate.

THE OLD COUNTRY

Europeans do not take water and electricity for granted like we do. When you walk into an apartment building in Copenhagen, or Paris, or Rome, you turn on the staircase light, which is on a timer. By the time you get to your landing, it switches off. However, timed lighting is not an exact science, and sometimes you are plunged into total darkness a few seconds before you reach your door. This can be jarring, and I never travel without a small flashlight in my purse.

The Europeans also have toilets with two different flush buttons: Press one for number one, press two for number two (and press zero for an operator). What a great idea. So simple, so logical—why didn't we think of that?

Not everything those foreigners do makes sense, though, like the bidet. This has got to be the silliest invention ever (along with the mini-vac, which doesn't really vac). In a bathroom that's usually so tiny that the shower is on a cord in the tub, why waste space and water on a fixture whose function is better accomplished by a washcloth?

And the Brits are a little too thrifty for my taste when it comes to central heating. The indoor temperature in England in September is the same as the outdoor temperature in Maine in December. This is true even in ritzy hotels like the Savoy, where I had to wear fleece-lined boots at night to go to the bathroom. We were being charged a king's ransom for two nights in the River Suite (someone else was paying), and I had to beg for a space heater.

Even when they're not in use, your appliances are still drawing electricity. Some noble souls unplug every machine that's idle, but I'm not about to keep bending down all day, plugging and unplugging. Nobody's perfect!

Lifestyle

PART

III

$1 Restaurants

I often picture myself as a guest on *Inside the Actors Studio*, and when James Lipton asks, "What is your favorite word?" my answer is, "Restaurant!" I would pay extra for a house without a kitchen. I love eating out. I love the whole ritual of studying the menu, hearing the specials, and sampling tastes of other people's dishes. I particularly love the fact that I can enjoy all this deliciousness without having done any of the work.

GO ETHNIC

Eating out doesn't have to break the bank or expand your waistline. My dream restaurant is a small family-run ethnic place where the chef is the owner's grandmother. The food is tasty, exotic, and cheap. Every city has these treasures. (If you live in an area where there is no immigrant population, I suggest you move.)

In Los Angeles alone, I've enjoyed fabulous Persian, Armenian, Polish, Greek, Cuban, and Thai feasts for less than twenty-five bucks, with enough leftovers for dinner the next two nights. That's actually cheaper than cooking at home. Many of these places don't have liquor licenses and allow you to bring your own wine or beer, which is another saving.

When our son got married in New York, we had to host a dinner for a gaggle of visiting Danes. We took seventeen people to a Vietnamese place in Chinatown and had a large variety of soups, spring rolls, seafood, chicken, and noodle dishes for a total cost of $250.

I've celebrated my birthday for the last few years by getting a private room in a Los Angeles Chinese restaurant. We invite a bunch of friends, plan the menu beforehand, and supply our own candles, flowers, and wine. We also bring in a portable CD player to create a mellow, jazzy ambience. It's a yummy spread for a dozen people that costs a few hundred bucks.

UNCHAIN MY HEART

I rarely eat fast food, junk food, or chain restaurant food, where every item—be it fish, meat, or fowl—is smothered with a gluey three-cheese melt. Sometimes I'm stuck in the boonies somewhere and TGIF is the only game in town. If so, I keep it simple and order the club sandwich rather than the "quick-fried crusty ravioli filled with pulled barbecue pork."

You won't catch me at a Red Lobster or Olive Garden. The ambiance is institutional, the prices aren't that terrific, and the food is blandly heavy heavy heavy. "Steak gorgonzola-alfredo" will put a lot of money in your cardiologist's pocket. Amusingly, I saw a paid ad on Olive Garden's home page that read, "Gastric Bypass Diet. Learn About Proper Dieting Following Gastric Bypass Surgery." I rest my case.

Discerning foodaholic that I am, I never thought I'd set foot in an IHOP until I spotted one of those discount coupons in the Sunday paper: "Order one entrée and get the second for free." That's an offer I couldn't refuse. My chicken fajita tostada salad was actually pretty good, and large enough for a family of four. So I started using coupons for other low-price chains: Souplantation, Sizzlers, Boston Market, and Acapulco, which were also a lot better than expected. I've been told by meat-loving friends that In-N-Out-Burger is the best chain in the Southwest. This is welcomed news, because my son and

I invested $600 in two different million-dollar home raffles last year, and all we won was a ten buck voucher at In-N-Out. That better be one terrific burger.

I am not a Starbucks aficionado: Four bucks for self-service coffee in a paper cup is not my idea of a good deal.

HELPFUL SITES FOR RESTAURANT ADDICTS

- OpenTable.com is free to join, and I often use it to make reservations. It's faster than calling, plus there's a savings plan. Each reservation gives you 100 points. When you reach 2,000, you get a twenty-dollar credit, so you're earning money while you eat.

- There's also Restaurant.com, where you pay ten bucks for a twenty-five-dollar restaurant voucher. I got so excited the day I joined that I ordered ten vouchers immediately. The next week they went on sale for half-price, and the two weeks after that they were down to two bucks. They keep repeating the same cycle, so I've learned to wait for the cheapest offering. Someone is paying me twenty-three dollars to eat out. That's a deal no frugalista could resista! The system isn't perfect, however. We bought a voucher for one restaurant that had gone out of business by the time we got there, and a few other places did not serve dinner— only breakfast and lunch, which was not stated on the voucher. These are minor flaws; it's still a great site.

- Chowhound.com is a site where foodies swap info on affordable restaurants all over the world. We used it when visiting Palm Springs, where we found a terrific Thai place.

OENOPHILE

Restaurants make more money on wine than food, so that bottle of Cab-Sav is way overpriced. I have a lawyer friend who actually has the guts to say, "I'll have your second cheapest bottle of Chardonnay." Note the choice of "second cheapest" rather than "cheapest." Classy!

I often call ahead to ask the restaurant's corkage fee. That's what they charge if you bring your own bottle. If the fee is fifteen dollars or less, it's a good deal; fancier places charge thirty bucks. Word to the wise: The waiter will look at your bottle and comment on the choice, so avoid embarrassment and leave the Thunderbird at home.

I can never resist any kind of buffet restaurant. Just the idea that I can have as much as I want of whatever I want thrills my greedy little self to the core. Lots of Indian and Thai places offer buffet lunches. Las Vegas now has many first-rate eateries, but I stick to those incredible all-you-can-grab buffets, where my brother-in-law once ate 2 pounds of shrimp cocktail at one sitting. Excessive, disgusting, but fun—once in a while.

HOITY-TOITY DINING

I occasionally splurge and enjoy an extra-fancy restaurant. Some places are a little too precious and serve concoctions that bear no resemblance to real food. I avoid them at all cost, not being a fan of squid-cheek mousse injected with watermelon sorbet.

But I do love fine dining, and a lot of swanky places have low-cost specials on certain days. In Los Angeles, for example:

• Jar has Mozzarella Monday.

• Campanile has Grilled Cheese Thursday.

• JiRaffe offers a twenty-four-dollar three-course meal with seven-dollar wine carafes on Mondays.

• Lucques has a thirty-five-dollar four-course Sunday dinner.

These special offerings are not just for peasants like me. I ran into Patricia Heaton (*Everybody Loves Raymond*), an old friend from acting class, at Campanile's Grilled Cheese Thursday.

Culinary schools often have terrific and affordable restaurants where Iron-Chefs-in-training develop their slicing and dicing skills. We tried the very elegant French Culinary Institute in Manhattan and had an excellent five-course prix fixe dinner: appetizer, fish, meat, salad, and dessert for forty-two dollars.

SWANKY SNOBS

I've had some extraordinary meals in first-class eateries, but there have been a few disasters. One night, we were at the Cannes film festival, and we were eating at the legendary Moulin de Mougins, full of Very Famous Movie Stars. We worked our way through endless dishes of butter, cream, and pig fat. Finally the snooty waiter brought a plate of little chocolate pastries, and I asked for a cup of coffee.

"I am sorree, Madame, but we serve ze café *after* les petit fours."

"Thank you, but I like my coffee *with* the dessert, please."

"Not posseeble."

"Couldn't you just make an exception this one little time?"

"Madame, I must inform you that in Frahnce, we do things differentlee from *your* countree."

I did not care for his tone.

"Right! We actually *fought* the Nazis!"

Very Famous Movie Stars stare as I am escorted out of the restaurant. We leave for home the next day, and I'm very happy to be back in the good old U. S. of A., where there are no rules.

Another time, we were at New York's celebrated Lutece. We were sitting at the bar, and I somehow managed to spill my aperitif as it was served to me. The bartender quickly gave me another—and charged us full price for the second drink.

At dinner, I saw a bug in my salad. The waiter removed the bowl, and I could have sworn the replacement was the original salad, minus the fly. I'm sure that fly would have gotten me ten free dinners at IHOP.

We had a much happier ending at Spago in Beverly Hills. Six of us had an 8 P.M. reservation. We were kept waiting at the bar until 9:30, then escorted to an indoor table, not the patio we had requested. Benni took the maître d' aside and firmly expressed his disappointment. As recompense, we were served a free bottle of champagne and Wolfgang Puck's signature smoked-salmon pizza, and we were moved to the patio for dessert after a spectacular dinner.

By the way, Spago has a unique way of dealing with doggy bags. If you want to take home your leftovers, they give you a number, and then you pick up your goodies at the exit. This way, you can avoid walking past all the rich and powerful mucky-mucks carrying a container with tomorrow's lunch.

Most upscale restaurants will give you a complimentary dessert if you mention it's someone's birthday. I suspect some folks pretend it's their birthday just to get the free slice of cake, but cheap as I am, I haven't yet sunk that low. I couldn't take the guilt of having the waiters serenade me while I was stealing from them.

$2 If You Have to Cook

I love making Thanksgiving dinner: I invite a dozen people, take a few days off, and wiggle my butt to *The Buena Vista Social Club* while I brine, baste, and braise from morning 'til night. My favorite part of this ritual is setting the table: I try to create a warm, welcoming atmosphere with vintage linens, glowing candles, and sparkling crystal. Once a year (or, more truthfully, once every few years) I am a domestic goddess.

EFFORT-LESS

Everyday food preparation is a rushed, harried, nerve-wracking chore that consumes time I'd rather spend at something more profitable. But we can't eat out every night—or so Benni claims—so I try to create meals that are quick, cheap, and healthful. The good news is that the most beneficial foods are also the least expensive. A curried tofu–veggie stir-fry costs a lot less than a roast leg of lamb, and it doesn't clog your arteries like the meat-and-potato diet I grew up with. The same goes for the linguine with pesto sauce that I make from my home-grown basil. Here are some lazy-ass recipes from my "I'd Rather Not Be Cooking" files.

- Foolproof guacamole: Mash an avocado with a container of fresh salsa.

- Spicy shrimp appetizer: Mix some ready-cooked shrimp with a container of fresh salsa.

- Meatloaf Acapulco: Mix a pound of ground turkey with a container of fresh salsa.

  Plus some suggestions from slothful friends:

- Gil's Garbage Gazpacho: Take yesterday's leftover salad and throw it in the food processor with a can of plum tomatoes. (I would add some fresh salsa.)

- Michael's Elegant Frozen Dessert: Mix some vanilla frozen yogurt in the processor with a ripe papaya (or mango, or pineapple). Add a little rum, and serve in wine glasses. (Skip the salsa in this one.)

> Whatever I prepare, I make sure there's enough for a few days. That's why coleslaw is my salad of choice: It's got staying power.

LOCAL HEROES

- I try to eat local and organic, which can be costly if you shop at classy emporiums like Whole Foods (better known as "Whole Paycheck"). I resent paying seven dollars for a pound of cherries.

- Trader Joe's is a much better deal, but there's an awful lot of plastic packaging, which means you're messing up the environment, and you're forced to buy four artichokes when you only need one. I prefer to buy my produce piece by piece, as I need it. This is not the American way. I once asked my neighborhood greengrocer for two shallots. He joked, "Two shallots? You expecting company?"

- Farmers' markets have glorious fruits and veggies, fresh and cheap, but you can only get things in season. Don't go looking for tomatoes in January.

- Of course, the freshest and cheapest is the home-grown stuff. Even city people can do a little gardening. I just visited a photojournalist in New York who had trays of herbs on her fire escape.

- Laura used to be Benni's assistant. She and her husband, Guillaume, are big meat eaters, but they want to avoid the chemically grown supermarket stuff. They found a nearby farm where the moo-moos live natural, happy lives. Half a beef was about $850, including butchering. They had meat for about two years.

Asian markets are the best places to buy fish. The product is fresher than fresh, and the prices are rock-bottom. Some of these places also sell live fowl, but that's a little too fresh for me.

SUPER-SIZED

I don't do those cavernous warehouse stores like Costco; they don't suit my lifestyle. Fifty pounds of sugar for twenty-two bucks may be a good deal, but I will probably be in the ground before I use 50 pounds of sugar.

I did score a 2-pound jar of mango chutney for $6.89, at Smart and Final. Unfortunately, it had the thick, glutinous consistency of cheap jam.

However, I am a big fan of the Ninety-Nine Cent Stores. I have found organic cauliflower and Silver Palate pasta sauces for—you guessed it—ninety-nine cents. And Italian pasta at two for a dollar. When you come across a great deal here, buy as much as you can squirrel away; it may not be there next week. I learned this the hard way, when they stopped carrying those round cardboard boxes of triangular cheese snacks that cost four bucks in the supermarket.

BRING IT HOME

When I don't feel like cooking the whole meal from scratch—which is most of the time—I pick up prepared foods like

- Sushi and salads from Whole Foods

- Roast lamb and poached salmon from Trader Joe's

- Chicken dinners from El Pollo Loco or Boston Market

- I also love Subway's tuna sub with all those veggies, but the clerks might not love me: I'm one of those calorie counters who asks them to scoop out the doughy part of the bread.

Just like with restaurants, small ethnic places are your best bet for inexpensive tasty takeout. I have enjoyed

- Barbecued eel from a Japanese market.

- Stuffed cabbage from a Russian deli.

- Lamb souvlaki from a Middle Eastern place.

I avoid those toxic supermarket delis, where the rancid macaroni salad has been trucked across the country in 100-gallon drums.

U.S. INGENUITY

Let us now praise that great American invention: food delivery. Europeans may feel superior to us in many ways, but if you can't pick up the phone on a cold, rainy night and have a hot, comforting dinner brought to your door, then you are not living in a civilized society. Yes, it's more expensive than making it yourself, but it lasts a few days, and during the time saved, you can sell stuff on eBay or write a book about thrifty living.

Expiration dates on canned and frozen foods such as "sell by, "best before," "best if used by," and "use by" are so confusing that I just use the smell-and-taste test for vintage groceries. Haven't died yet.

There are people who save a bundle by purchasing outdated food from the supermarket. I do not suggest this for meat, fish, or dairy products. Frugal is one thing; nuts is something else.

IN VERITAS VINO

When it comes to wine, I have a lucky handicap for a bargainista: It appears that my taste buds are so underdeveloped that I cannot tell the difference between a $200 Vérité La Muse Sonoma County 2004 and a bottle of Trader Joe's "Two-Buck Chuck" (Charles Shaw).

I also can't tell the difference between white wine and turpentine. Baron de Rothschild supposedly said, "The only time to drink white wine is when there's no red available." I'm with him. I have occasionally enjoyed a glass of fruity white Zinfandel, which, to a serious oenophile, is about as sophisticated as Welch's grape juice.

I've tried many times to educate my palate. I've visited vineyards, attended wine tastings, and even took a class, all to no avail. If it's red and not too acidic, I'll happily drink it, often as a spritzer, mixed with club soda, which is about as déclassé as you can get.

I was at a swanky dinner party and, when I thought no one was looking, poured a few drops of seltzer into my glass of burgundy. I was nailed by the wine Nazi sitting next to me, who screamed, "That's like murdering a baby!" Can't take me anywhere.

We buy our wines at Trader Joe's, home of the infamous "Two-Buck Chuck." I also favor a chain called Bevmo. They just had a sale on Beringer's cabernet for $3.99 a bottle. We usually pay around seven dollars, so we bought a case. Should have gotten more; it's almost gone, and the sale is over.

For bubbly occasions, I serve Prosecco. It's way cheaper than champagne, and I like anything Italian better than anything French.

PASSING WATER

A true thriftaholic never follows the herd, and I refuse to waste money on bottled water. It's one of the biggest rip-offs around, and those noxious plastic bottles are an ecological disaster. Dasani, owned by Coca-Cola, is filtered municipal tap water. Pepsi owns Aquafina, which is also municipal water.

I bought a home water test kit on eBay for twenty bucks, and we passed with flying colors. I use a filter to improve the flavor and thumb my nose at the corporate giants, just like my hero, Erin Brockovich!

Let Me Entertain You

$3

ALL YOU NEED IS LOVE

I have a friend I see only when she's a guest in my house. She's delighted to be invited over, but she never reciprocates or even invites me to lunch. This one-way street happens a lot when married people have single friends. Folks who live solo assume that no one expects them to be hospitable. Wrong! People like a little payback once in a while, especially petty, small-minded people like me.

My friend whined that, since her divorce, she had downsized from a large home to a small apartment, and she was embarrassed to have guests in such cramped quarters. This is a lame excuse because, as my immigrant mother used to say, "When there's room in the heart, there's room in the house."

Benni was producing a movie in Belgrade, and his leading actor invited us to spend an evening in his home. This "home" turned out to be one crowded room in his mother-in-law's apartment. He lived in that tiny space with his wife and baby. We still managed to eat, drink, and be merry.

Giving a great party is not really about the elegance of the surroundings, the quality of the menu, or the vintage of the wine. I've been bored to death at glamorous Beverly Hills banquets. You can provide a fun evening for friends as long as you have generosity of spirit and a little imagination. I myself have neither of those qualities, but I've managed to have some successful get-togethers just by making the effort.

FRUGAL FUN

Hosting a party can be a challenge for the thriftaholic, but there are always ways to cut corners. Before dinner, we generally make a large quantity of one mixed drink, which costs less than offering a full bar, and the colors of sliced fruit floating in a pretty glass pitcher are inviting. I like kir royales, or margaritas, or, in summer, Campari with grapefruit juice. Of course, there's always some guy who is happy only with straight-up bourbon, and we grudgingly accommodate him.

One-dish meals are economical. They may not be the most sophisticated foods, but I see nothing wrong with serving lasagna, chili, or lamb stew. I also love a curried chicken concoction called Country Captain, the first dish I ever learned to make from *The Joy of Cooking*. I do not favor bland casseroles like that classic fifties tuna, noodle, and potato chip combo. However, I have one friend who was brought up with that dish, and to her it represents mother love.

I'm not a big fan of the all-American barbecue, but Benni loves hot dogs, so for his birthday I got an inexpensive assortment of Italian, Polish, and German sausages and invited a gang over. We called the party Benni's Sausage Celebration, which, of course, inspired countless predictable jokes ("I'd like to propose a toast to Benni's sausage!"). In honor of the birthday boy, I served the traditional Danish condiments: mustard, ketchup, rémoulade sauce, crispy fried onions, chopped raw onions, and cucumber salad, a novel change from relish and kraut. There were lots of giggles as we taught everyone the unpronounceable Danish words for each item. (It's been said that Danish is not a language; it's a throat disease.)

Brunches cost a lot less than dinner parties. Whether it's French toast, a Spanish omelet, or a tofu–veggie scramble, brunch ingredients are not expensive, and they're easy to assemble. And, ideally, not much alcohol is consumed. Afterward, you've got the whole rest of the day to relax with the Sunday puzzle.

BYOB, AND SOMETHING TO EAT

Potluck get-togethers are another cheapo way to have fun with friends. I do a Women's Day celebration every year for about twenty-five gal-pals. It's a garden lunch, and everyone brings something to eat or drink. I never give assignments, because I resent it when someone invites me and says, "Could you please bring two bottles of champagne and make a crème brûlée for twelve?" That's not potluck; that's badluck.

Instead, I just tell everyone to bring what they like but to let me know their choice beforehand so that we don't end up with five cheesecakes. It always turns into a sumptuous buffet, and I hand out recycled takeout containers at the end so everyone goes home with a free meal.

I get the ball rolling by going around the table and having everyone introduce herself. After that, we spend a happy afternoon complaining about the state of the world, complaining about our work, complaining about our husbands, complaining about not having a husband, and admiring each other's outfits. We know how to have a good time.

DETAILS, NOT DOLLARS

When it comes to setting the table, a little imagination goes a long way. My friend Lehang is known for the inventiveness of her low-cost parties. Once, she made an Indonesian feast for ten people. The table was covered with dark green banana leaves, which substituted for a tablecloth and plates: We ate right off the leaves. It was fun and exotic.

Another time, she gave a serene poolside lunch using only white: white tablecloths, white floral arrangements, and an improvised canopy of billowing white sheets. She got the sheets for a few bucks at a yard sale and bought hugely discounted roses and lilies at the wholesale flower market. Most cities have these markets; just look on the Internet. Lehang's spectacular budget parties have always been a labor of love. Now word of her talent has gotten out, and people are hiring her as an event planner.

One thing I've learned from the Danes is the potent effect of candlelight. A dining room that is lit only by candles has a magical ambiance. I buy boxes of tapers and tea lights at rummage sales for almost nothing.

I often put a tiny gift on each plate, just some little item that I've picked up on the cheap somewhere: a brass bookmark, a vintage letter opener, whatever I can find. Everybody likes to be coddled, and it doesn't take a lot of money to make each guest feel special.

PERSON TO PERSON

The real fun of any party is connecting with other people. There's nothing worse than going to a shindig where you barely know anyone and leaving the party in the same isolated state. The party giver's job is to make introductions between the guests, and the best way to do that is to hook up people with similar interests. "Terry, this is Alex. You guys have a lot in common. Alex also collects Nazi memorabilia."

My friend Bob celebrated sudden wealth by inviting 360 people on a private Caribbean cruise. The journey had four legs: Each week ninety guests would disembark, and the next group would get on board. These were all accomplished, creative individuals, and there was a sprinkling of celebrities. When we arrived, we personally knew about fifteen out of the ninety.

Bob had a brilliant plan for connecting strangers: a salon. Every night before dinner, we would all gather in the lounge, and various guests would offer a lecture or a performance, show a film, read a short story, give a tango class, a cooking demonstration, whatever. Benni became a big star. He entertained us with puzzles and games, which included levitating Francis Ford Coppola. The salon was a great way to break the ice, and by the end of the week, we were one big happy family. Many people who started out as strangers formed lasting friendships. This was a host who knew how to do his job.

LET THE GAMES BEGIN

I was so impressed with the salon format that I tried to introduce it to my closest social circle. No such luck: My scuzzy friends would rather just eat, drink, and play poker. At birthdays, however, we do get creative. We eat, drink, and roast the celebrant with funny songs and poems. And then we play poker.

In fact, game nights are a popular form of free fun in my highly competitive posse. We'll get together for an evening of Boggle, Charades, or Pictionary. I won't say I enjoy every minute. I'm a Boggle champ, but nobody wants me on their Pictionary team; all my pathetic attempts at drawings look like Rorschach tests.

One event I will never host is a New Year's Eve bash. I'm still suffering from post-traumatic stress from my last attempt. Years ago, in New York, I invited around twenty people to ring out the old. What I forgot was that people wander from party to party on New Year's. Guests kept dropping in and out all evening, so I never had more than four at any one time. At midnight, there was one lonely soul who was so bored that he fell asleep on the couch. At 1:30, a crowd of revelers rang the bell. I pretended I was in bed and did not answer the door. Never again!

At a holiday party Kathy, a dance teacher, made an unusual contribution. She created a dance tape and brought a variety of percussion instruments: bongos, tambourines, triangles, castanets, maracas, and so on. Banging out Latin rhythms was a great release from the daily grind, but you can have this kind of fun only if you are in contact with your inner child. Since my entire life is ruled by my inner child, I had no problem with it.

One of the most original parties we ever attended was actually a wedding present. Our hosts had received a gift of a private wine-tasting seminar, and they invited a dozen friends to participate. An expert gave us a lecture and tastes of twelve different wines, each accompanied by food. It was fun and informative. This wedding present, needless to say, was not a gift you could find at a yard sale.

$4 Tripping

IT'S A NOT-SO-WONDERFUL LIFE

Some people think of travel as a luxury; I say it's a necessity. I've always felt great pity for George Bailey in *It's a Wonderful Life*. I know most folks find Frank Capra's Christmas film stirring and heartwarming and inspirational. To me, it's a horror flick.

You see, I grew up in the Bronx, and I felt like if I didn't get away I'd bust. So I understand George Bailey's restlessness. "I'm shakin' the dust of this crummy little town off my feet, and I'm gonna see the world. Italy, Greece, the Parthenon, the Coliseum."

Instead, poor old George takes the tedious job in the shabby office, lives in the chilly old house he always hated, and watches life pass him by. He sacrifices his dreams for the sake of people he loves. At least he had the dreams. There are actually dreamless people who happily choose to live every day of their lives in the place they were born.

When we had a country house, I asked our elderly neighbor when he had last visited New York. "Never been out of the county," he said proudly. We're talking about a two-hour drive to the greatest city in the world, and this bozo didn't have the teensiest bit of curiosity about it. Am I being too much of a big-city snob when I call that a limited world view? So be it.

Travel costs money, but I've always found ways to budgetize my trips. For starters, I never take tours. Too expensive, plus I don't like being told where to eat, which museum to visit, and what time to get up in the morning. I'm a control freak who needs to be in charge of my own plans—just ask Benni. Also, I'm horrified at the thought of being thrown together with a busload of random yahoos. I'd rather choose my own yahoos, thank you very much.

LOST IN TRANSLATION

Planning a trip is half the fun, but it has its challenges. When you come to a foreign language Web site and hit "Translate This Page," the results can be bewildering:

- "The atmosphere to Heaven is a comfortable and refined farm with suggestive apartments furnished and equipped with all comfort."

- "Immersed in panoramic swimming pool with salt water can regenerate prejudice to admire one of the territories most characteristic and beautiful in the world."

I'm intrigued by the idea of a "suggestive apartment"; not sure I want to "regenerate prejudice," though.

I also consult guidebooks, written in real English, that I pick up at library sales, and I might order something essential from Amazon, like Frommer's *Tuscany & Umbria's Best-Loved Driving Tours*. I found a used copy for eighty-four cents, plus four bucks for shipping.

On a family visit to the ancient port village of Rome, Ostia Antica, we decided to splurge and hire a guide, but none were available. So our son, who's a history buff, whipped out his map and guidebook and gave us an instructional tour for the excellent price of zero.

THE REAL DEAL

I prefer bed and breakfasts to conventional hotels. They're a lot cheaper and a lot cozier, and you make a lot more contact with the natives, which is one of the great pleasures of traveling. (When you stay at a Four Seasons, there's not much chance of hanging out with the owners.)

At a B & B in Auckland, our hosts invited us to join them and their friends at the local pub. We had a little trouble with the New Zealand slang, which all sounds like baby-talk: "brolly" for umbrella, "Chrissy" for Christmas, and the like. But we still had a fun, authentic experience that could never have happened at a Hilton—or a "Hilly," as I guess the Kiwis would say.

In Japan we stayed at a traditional country inn, where we survived a monsoon in a building with paper walls. I won't say it was enjoyable, but it sure as hell was authentic.

DOWN ON THE FARM

My favorite bargain lodgings are the *agriturismos* of Italy. These are beautifully located working farms and vineyards that rent a few rooms to tourists. Some offer only breakfast, others include sumptuous dinners. All the ingredients, including the wine and the olive oil, are usually organic and produced on the property. If there is a heaven, it's gotta be a lot like an Italian *agriturismo*.

One farm we discovered in our wanderings was La Riserva Montebello. It consists of some ancient stone buildings near the medieval lake town of Bolsena, a two-and-a-half-hour drive north of Rome.

When we arrived, there were two bottles of the house wine—one red, one white—welcoming us to a room furnished with charming antiques. Rustic decals were painted on the walls, and just outside the door was a small terrace overlooking spectacular Lake Bolsena: an auspicious beginning.

Nothing is perfect, however: The bath towels were as thin as dishcloths. Since then, I've learned to pack my own terry bath sheet—no big deal.

There were two spring-fed swimming pools. ("Spring-fed" means freezing, but fresh and invigorating. Italians don't heat their pools, just as the English don't heat their homes.)

We enjoyed archery, ping-pong, and beautiful strolls along the farm paths, with visits to the barnyard animals. One day we were walking in the woods and came across the owner's girlfriend filling up a basket with mushrooms. That evening, the first course at dinner was wild mushrooms sautéed with olive oil and garlic, a splendid testimony to the local food movement.

We could drive ten minutes to Bolsena or twenty minutes to the splendid city of Orvieto. For serious sightseeing, the clean, punctual train from Orvieto to Rome takes an hour and ten minutes.

All these activities were a pleasant way of killing time between the really important events of the day: the meals. The breakfast buffet consisted of:

- Homemade yogurt

- Homegrown fruit

- A variety of breads and cakes

- Local cheeses

- Various cereals, jams, and honey

- Eggs boiled to order

- Ham, salami, and prosciutto home cured from the farm's own pigs. This gave me a moment's pause because we had enjoyed our contact with the animals, but at least they had lived a good life.

Dinner began with an aperitif on the terrace—either a glass of Prosecco or the house red mixed with a little fruit juice, a postmodern sangria. Olives, salami, cheese, and nuts were also offered, which we munched on while gazing at the sun setting over the lake.

The meal was served in a romantic candle-lit dining room. This was a leisurely, two-hour affair with at least four courses. The menu changed every day. Here's a typical dinner:

- Mixed bruschetta

- Gnocchi with meat sauce

- Salad

- Grilled lake fish with parsley and lemon sauce and mashed potatoes

- Tiramisu

- Fruit and cheese

The feast was enhanced by several wines and after-dinner liqueurs.

Since there are only a dozen guest rooms, the intimate atmosphere allowed for friendly contact. There was the Norwegian wedding party, which we mistook for a funeral because everyone was so quiet and somber. And the Republican lawyers from San Diego who had never heard of Jon Stewart but who offered to lend us some fleece vests on a chilly evening. And the Dutch minister who was on his way to Israel to study Hebrew.

We got friendly with Marco, the gentleman farmer who owns the property. He invited us for a ride in his vintage Lotus convertible and promised to show us his modern art collection on our next visit.

When we checked out, Marco insisted on giving us four bottles of wine to take home.

The daily charge for all this bliss bliss bliss, including food and wine, was a little over $200 for two people. The only thing cheaper would have been camping, and that's not this baby's idea of a good time. Viva l'Italia!

$5 More Tripping

AIRBORNE

The most expensive and least enjoyable part of travel is getting there. The Internet is full of sites that will lead you to cheap tickets and last-minute deals. Here are a few other money-saving suggestions:

- Travel Tuesdays or Wednesdays. These are the slow days for the airlines. I always try to avoid Sundays, which are the busiest. If we're traveling coach, we reserve the aisle and window, hoping that no one will want the middle seat. I've sometimes thought of showing up in surgical masks to discourage anyone from sitting next to us, but I don't have the guts.

- Travel in the off-season. Not only are flights cheaper, but so are hotels. September and October are my favorite times to travel. The weather is pleasant, the tour buses are gone, and the grapes are being harvested.

- Look for unexpected airline routes. Air India's nonstop flight to Hamburg from Los Angeles is $400 cheaper than Lufthansa on certain days. (This would be a good deal for some people. I, however, would expect someone to pay *me* to go Hamburg.)

- Consult a travel agent. It costs nothing, and they often have inside information not available to the general public.

There's a famous *Seinfeld* episode where Elaine is stuck in coach next to an obnoxious gum-chewing lady. I played that lady, and I know just how Elaine felt. Coach is hell, and I try to avoid it at all cost. I find cheap flights, then use my mileage for upgrades. This is easier said than done. We were trying to get from L.A. to Rome on my American Airlines mileage. The best they could offer was for us to fly coach to Chicago, wait four hours to connect to an upgraded flight, and then return home by way of Istanbul. I don't think so.

PACK RAT

I am an obsessive packer, and I hate myself for it. I start around two weeks before taking off, and I'm still at it until the last minute, even if we're just going away for the weekend. It takes me a day to sort out and organize toiletries and cosmetics and half a day to pick the right socks. I wish I could be one of those people who just throw things into a bag at the last minute. Not gonna happen. I cannot bear the idea of not having what I need when I need it.

- What if it rains and I don't have an umbrella?

- What if we get romantic and I don't have sexy lingerie?

- What if I chip my nail and I don't have polish?

Besides the inconvenience of missing something essential, the main reason for my wacky-packy compulsion is frugality. I simply cannot bear the thought of having to go out and pay full price in an expensive foreign shop for something I have a dozen of at home, for which I paid fifty cents each. That's exactly what happened when I neglected to pack a warm sweater for Venice, where they don't have thrift stores.

I used to collect expensive, high-quality Hartmann luggage, which I picked up cheaply at yard sales. I've since switched to ordinary nondescript suitcases, because fancy bags are much more vulnerable to thievery. Now my bags blend in so well with everyone else's that I have trouble recognizing them; I keep pulling someone else's luggage off the carousel.

GETTING AROUND

- In Europe, just like at home, public transportation is your best bet, beginning with your arrival. A cab from Heathrow into London would have cost a hundred bucks! Instead, we took the underground, which was actually above ground for most of the way. It brought us a few blocks from our destination. We've also taken the train from Kastrup airport in Copenhagen to my sister-in-law's house in the suburbs. Of course, these were short stays, so we each had one small carry-on bag. When we have our usual four bulging suitcases, trains are not an option.

- One of my worst travel experiences was spending three days in Paris with a car. The traffic and parking were unpleasant, time-consuming, and costly. We would have been a lot better off on the Metro.

- Sometimes being frugal can backfire: We decided not to spend the extra money on a GPS system on our Italian rental car and boy, did we regret it! We were headed for an *agriturismo* that was located about an hour south of Milan. Benni was the driver, and I was the navigator. I learned something on that trip: I learned that I cannot read maps. We left Milan, and after three confusing hours getting nowhere, we realized that we were going north, not south. The giveaway was the line of uniformed guards as we approached the Swiss border. Not a happy day.

WHERE TO STAY

- You can save a lot of money if you're willing to forgo the convenience of being right in the center of town. We were going to spend five days in Rome, and there were no hotels under $200 a night. We decided to stay in a little seaside suburb called Fregene. We took the commuter train into Rome every day, which took about forty minutes. Our pleasant hotel room cost eighty bucks, including breakfast.

- My friend Mimi organized a family reunion for fifteen people by renting a castle in southern France for a week. It was a lot cheaper than a hotel, and they took turns making dinner. Part of the fun was buying fresh eggs, cheese, and produce from the local farmers. With a long cocktail hour and haphazard organization, dinner often wasn't ready until 10 P.M., but late dining is customary in that part of the world, so they fit right in.

- Couchsurfing.com links travelers to private homes all over the world. You might get a bedroom, a sofa, or just a patch of floor, but your host will give you genuine insights into local culture, and the price is incredibly free. I heard about one American student who got along with her Lisbon host so well that she stayed for three months.

- George and Alice, my old college pals, go hiking in New Zealand every year. They are out in the wilderness all day, then just take a brief shower before going out to dinner, so they have no need for all the bells and whistles of a fancy hotel. Instead, they stay at a hostel and pay extra for a private room with bath. This costs a whopping forty-five dollars a night. It sounds like a fabulous vacation—except for the hiking part. Instead, I think I'll try the hostel in Barcelona.

AFFORDABLE EATS

Even when the dollar is weak, there's always a bargain to be found. I spend a lot of time in Copenhagen, one of the most expensive cities in Europe, where it's not uncommon for a restaurant dinner to cost between $50 and $100 per person. But like most European cities, Copenhagen has an immigrant working-class population that provides cheap and delicious ethnic food.

My favorite is a Turkish buffet in the center of town called Ankara. It offers a staggering selection of thirty dishes for nine dollars, and they have a patio for outdoor dining. Nine dollars would barely be enough for a cappuccino in the average Danish restaurant.

LAND OF THE LIVING

I've been to lots of faraway places, and after years of respectfully visiting every museum, castle, and church in the guidebooks, I suddenly began to feel that everything around me was—how can I say it—dead, except for the hordes of tourists. So I raced out of the Gothic cathedral and into the supermarket, and I've never turned back.

It's not that I don't appreciate viewing art and architecture and history, but a cheaper, more authentic experience can be had by wandering through markets, pharmacies, and hardware stores. My house is full of foreign loot, like my collection of super-realistic plastic sushi I picked up in Tokyo's restaurant supply district, my Florentine cheese grater, and my midcentury Danish Modern toilet brush, the first ever designed to fit into a molded holder.

> Discount theater tickets are available in New York, London, and other theater-friendly cities. The best time to go the half-price ticket booth on Broadway is Tuesday evening or any major Jewish holiday. Benni and I got aisle seats for *Hair* on the first night of Passover. Generally, Yom Kippur is your best bet.
>
> Also, you can call the Metropolitan Opera at noon to reserve senior tickets for twenty bucks.

More importantly, I've gotten real insights into culture—theirs and ours—by just soaking up everyday commerce. Like the time in Stockholm when the raggedy old man in front of me in the checkout line bought ten cans of beer and a potato because the liquor laws in Sweden required you to buy food whenever you got booze. Hey, we should try this! How about a law that says every time you buy a ticket for an action movie, you also have to buy a novel written by a woman?

In Cannes, I went to the local farmers' market to buy fruit and cheese for a cheapo picnic lunch. There I saw French women, young and old, all wearing teeny mini-skirts and sky-high stiletto heels, with bare legs. They click-clacked along those bumpy cobblestone streets without dropping a baguette. (They wore those same stilettos at the beach, along with topless bikinis.)

I, on the other hand, dress for comfort when I travel, so I was the town frump in my elastic-waist jeans. I was also wearing Easy Spirit sneakers with "Extra cushioning and a breathable foot pad" so that I could walk easily, which didn't help: I still kept turning my ankles on those damn cobblestones.

My happiest offbeat tourist moment took place in an upscale suburb of Copenhagen, when Nina, my sister-in-law, asked if I'd like to visit the garbage dump. Yes, you heard me, the garbage dump. But remember, Denmark has a progressive social system. This was no nasty, smelly landfill but a neat and tidy trash depot on a pleasant woodsy road.

And the kicker was, they had this large wooden shed where people put perfectly good things that they were simply tired of, and anyone could just take what they wanted. A frugalista's dream! I walked off with an embroidered tablecloth and the huge '60s orange teapot that's on the book cover. Now that's my idea of recycling.

It doesn't cost a dime to gawk at the fish heads for sale in Chinatown or to see the entire staff bow in formal welcome when a Tokyo department store opens in the morning, so my brand of tourism is great for people on a budget or those who, like me, are just plain cheap. I've had priceless cultural experiences that couldn't have happened in museums. I'm all for art, but there's something to be said for visiting the town dump.

PUMPED UP

My old friend Tana is a documentary filmmaker, which means she does not have a fat bank account, but her lifelong dream has been to visit every exotic corner of the world—the more remote, the better. She has been to the Amazon, Antarctica, Mongolia, the Middle East, and Africa, and she gets paid for it: She works for specialized travel companies as a guide. (It helps that she speaks several languages.)

She's had many spectacular adventures on her journeys, but she's also seen a lot of poverty and hardship. In one African village, the women had to walk for miles every day to collect water. Back home in New York, Tana had a "pump party" and raised enough money to donate a mechanical pump to the villagers, who now have precious clean water available for the first time in their lives. They had a huge ceremonial celebration when the pump was installed, and they named it "Tana."

DO-GOOD TRAVEL

If you're financially secure but want a trip with a deeper purpose than eating, drinking, shopping, and sightseeing, you can spend your vacation helping the poor, usually on a building project. Habitat for Humanity, United Way, and many other philanthropic organizations offer community service vacations. My show-biz friends Penny and Barry spent three weeks helping to rebuild New Orleans. (You don't have to leave the country to find people in need.)

I also know two retired academics, Gil and Shirley, who volunteer through Global Volunteers to teach English abroad every summer. So far, these goodwill ambassadors have given classes in Italy, Crete, and Portugal.

Global Exchange is another organization that sends teachers to foreign countries.

I've performed all over the world, so I've been lucky enough to travel at someone else's expense. The best was a booking in Sydney that got me two first-class tickets with stops in Auckland and Oahu. Shooting a commercial in Buffalo was not quite as thrilling, but I still get a kick out of ordering room service on someone else's dime.

Free Entertainment

$6

HITTING THE STACKS

Public libraries are great venues for free entertainment. Not only do they offer books, magazines, CDs, videos, and Internet access, but they have lectures, exhibits, classes, and special events for kids. Libraries are the biggest cultural bargain around.

I take advantage of the system right in my home office. Let's say I read a review of a novel that sounds interesting; this is usually a psychological mystery written by a woman that takes place in a gloomy English village. I just reserve it online, and my local branch contacts me when the book is available. Easy as pie. (An expression I've never really understood: What's so easy about pie? I think pie is difficult.)

You can often find free outdoor movie screenings during the summer. One such venue in Los Angeles is the Hollywood Forever cemetery, which is the resting place of Cecil B. DeMille, Rudolph Valentino, and many other show-biz luminaries.

GROUP READS

Many of my friends belong to book clubs. This is a great way to combine intellectual stimulation with snacks. It's not for me, though, because some of the choices are nonfiction, and I have very little interest in the real world.

One day I'm going to organize a Shakespeare book club. I've read and seen many of the plays, but I always feel that I'm missing a lot of it, especially the jokes: There are too many puns based on unfamiliar words. I need help.

MUSEUM MUSINGS

Every museum has one free night a week. Also, most people don't realize that when there is a charge, it is often optional. My Danish niece was in New York and invited a group of us to the Museum of Natural History for the big lizard show. We were six adults and four kids, and I saw her hesitate when she saw the suggested ticket prices of ten dollars for adults and six bucks for children. I pointed to the word *suggested* and explained that she could pay what she could afford, which she did.

As it turned out, we never even got to see the lizards because the lines were too long. Instead, we strolled around the permanent collection, then browsed through the gift shop, which is always a highlight of any museum visit, along with the café.

The next day, I went to the Metropolitan Museum of Art with my old college friend Sheila. Again, the admission fee was optional, but we chose to pay the full price because there were only two of us, and we wanted to support the institution. I'm not always as cheap as you might think.

Galleries are a great freebie for art lovers. You can put yourself on a gallery's mailing list and get invited to openings. If you don't care for the current exhibit of grotesque fat ladies, there's always the free wine and cheese and terrific people watching; artsy types wear the most interesting jewelry.

If you favor a particular museum, then it pays to become a member. I live near the Los Angeles County Museum of Art (LACMA). My membership costs ninety dollars a year, for which I get two free tickets any time I go, plus invitations to all kinds of special events and discounts in the fabulous gift shop.

Many museums offer free concerts. LACMA has jazz in the atrium on Fridays. You sit outdoors, sip a glass of wine, and snap your fingers to some Dixieland—a pleasant way to end the week.

A DAY AT THE BEACH

There's plenty of free fun on a beach. We have a group that gets together on occasional Sundays for Pacific Ocean volleyball. I do not participate in any activity that involves running after a flying object, but I do like to breathe the sea air, look for shells, spot dolphins, and then join all the players for a sunset picnic. Of course, the traffic and parking are a pain, but it's still a pretty relaxing low-cost day.

SUNDAY IN THE PARK

A park is a peaceful, happy place: a green, calm oasis in the middle of stressful urban life. It's also a good barometer of the local culture. The first thing I noticed in Copenhagen was the number of topless sunbathers. In a country with a gray, wet climate, sunny days are too precious to waste on such trivialities as modesty. I was meandering through one of these parks with my then-teenage son, and I can't count the number of times he walked into a tree; his attention was elsewhere.

Parks are also great for free cultural events, such as rock concerts and operas, in addition to the wandering buskers (street performers), who are often first class. We've enjoyed everything from jugglers to break dancers.

SUBWAY SERENADE

Street performers are not just in the parks. Once a tourist came up to me and asked if it was safe to enter the subway at Grand Central Station. It was around 2 P.M. on a weekday, and I assured him he was in no danger.

About ten minutes later, I myself ran down to catch a train and there, on the platform, was a rainbow coalition of Juilliard students playing a sublime Mozart string quartet. I often wonder about that tourist and what he told people about New York when he got home.

You can join a free walking tour in many cities here and in Europe. Just search for them—and everything else—on Google. I live on Planet Google.

IF YOU BUILD IT, THEY WILL COME

Some new buildings are terrific examples of cutting-edge modern architecture, and they have lobbies, courtyards, and gardens that are open to the public. Even if you don't have tickets for Disney Hall in Los Angeles, simply wandering around the Frank Gehry edifice is awe inspiring.

STREET PEOPLE

I love street fairs. They have food, they have bargain shopping, and they often have musicians, so you get a concert while munching on a funnel cake. I once stopped to listen to a fabulous Latin band at a fair on Manhattan's Upper West Side. The music was so exhilarating, the rhythms so irresistible, that the crowd broke into a spontaneous salsa party.

The leader of the band was an older, white-haired gentleman, and I was so impressed with the quality of this unknown group that I was about to ask if he needed help getting representation. I saved myself a lot of embarrassment when I noticed the bandleader's name on a banner: Tito Puente. For free! At a street fair!

DEAD AND ALIVE

This may sound morbid, but I've attended a few show-biz funerals, and they were the best show in town. The speeches were funny, poignant, and literate, and there were great musical performances. Celebrity memorials are joyous celebrations, and they are often open to the public.

My son was lucky enough to be at the memorial service for folk singer Odetta. He got to hear Harry Belafonte, Joan Baez, Pete Seeger, Peter Yarrow, and a sixty-seven-year-old country blues singer from Tennessee named Rattlesnake Annie.

There are free spoken word events all over the place. I go to one in L.A. called Sit 'n Spin, where writer–performers read personal essays, and there's always a live band. The pieces are sometimes funny, sometimes filthy, sometimes shocking, like the essays by my friend Andrea, who is surprisingly entertaining while describing her incestuous relationship with her daddy. There's also Maggie, who went from being a fundamentalist Christian to a pole dancer. You will not read this material in a family newspaper, which is what makes it so much fun.

Of course, you have to use your judgment on this one. It might not be too cool to invite someone to a free funeral on a first date.

COURTSHIP

Phyllis is a judge. We became friends when she was still a divorce lawyer and a single mom. She had just started seeing Bernie, a law professor (whom she eventually married). Their idea of a hot date was to spend the evening in night court. I wonder if it was as much fun as *Boston Legal*.

HOLIDAY MADNESS

Public holidays offer many opportunities for free fun—for other people. I'm claustrophobic, so you wouldn't catch me in that Times Square mob on New Year's Eve. However, I did attend a village Fourth of July parade in the country. Leading the marchers was the town barber dressed as Santa Claus. I'm still trying to figure that one out.

SENIOR MOMENTS

Senior centers offer a lot of free and low-cost activities, from tai chi classes to line dancing. My friend Mimi gets two-dollar tickets for Broadway shows. However, in order to qualify as a member of the center, she is obliged to eat there three times a week. It sounds a little depressing, but she joined with a group of friends, so they meet up for bland food and lively gossip. The lunches cost one dollar; you can also get breakfast for fifty cents. Maybe *socialism* isn't such a dirty word after all!

If you're lucky enough to live near a college or university, there are lots of free cultural events going on. For example, Columbia University has lunchtime concerts. Princeton has a lecture series with speakers like Joan Didion and Mario Vargas Llosa.

Churches have all kinds of free fun. The Cathedral of St. John the Divine in Manhattan has symphonic concerts, jazz recitals, and the annual blessing of the animals, where you can watch a procession of wild and crazy pets like camels, tortoises, and llamas. I wonder if you can also get them to curse animals, like the weevils in my pantry.

A GIFT FROM WALT

I'm not a big fan of theme parks (except for Sea World—Sea World rocks!). I hate the rides, the junk food, and the long lines, and all the ho-ho-ho fake cheeriness makes me gag. I also hate the sinfully expensive admission prices. One adult ticket at Disneyland costs a whopping sixty-nine bucks! But you can get in free on your birthday if you register online in advance at www.disneyland.com. Just think of how much you could save if everyone in your family had the same birthday!

If you ever have to spend time at an airport, the international arrival building is a terrific free show because you can observe the human drama of family reunions. Jonathan's friend Adrian happened to be there when a planeload of Chinese orphans arrived to be united with their adoptive families. Adrian still gets weepy when she talks about it. I still get weepy when I think about it.

The Parent Trap

KIDS ARE US

In Denmark, my country-in-law, there is low-cost child care for every child, starting in infancy. This includes an occasional camp holiday in the country. The state also takes care of all your kid's dental and medical needs, and education is free from kindergarten on up. At the university level, students are paid a modest living wage to encourage them to stay in school. (I have a nephew who has spent the last five years getting a doctorate in philosophy, and he's in no hurry to finish.) If your child has a physical or mental handicap, the state will provide for him all his life. Of course, all these progressive social benefits are paid for by sky-high taxes, but most Danes feel they are getting a lot of bang for their bucks.

It's a little different in the States. When my son, Jonathan, was little, he used to ask me why he didn't have any brothers or sisters, and I would say, "We didn't have more children because we got the one we wanted." This was almost true. What I left out was that kids cost money. They demand pricey things like babysitters, and college, and braces.

SITTING PRETTY

I solved the child care issue by giving piano lessons at home when Jono was little, and my parents lived nearby. For a few years I had a series of young Scandinavian women staying with me as au pairs. Two were angels, and two were psychopaths, but even the good ones needed mothering. One lovely Swedish girl decided to lose weight by going on a carrot diet. I had to put a stop to it when her face turned orange.

We all know that grandparents are the best babysitters, and the price is right. My sister-in-law, Nina, lives in the same suburb as her married daughters, so the grandkids just bike over for visits. I live 3,000 miles away from my son, so if he has children I will not enjoy the privileges of an extended family. I'm very sad about this: Who's going to be there to warn the grandchild how dangerous the world is?

DOLLARS, BUT NO SENSE

Raising a child is an expensive proposition, but money doesn't necessarily lead to good parenting.

- I sometimes take a look at "The Real Housewives of Someplace-or-Other" just for the sheer pleasure of feeling superior. One mother took her two surly teenage girls to the mall and spent $1,800 on seven pieces. These were not prom dresses; they were everyday items. One of the girls was still surly, however, because she didn't know for sure if she was going to get a BMW for her eighteenth birthday.

- An affluent mother on one of those wife-swapping reality shows had three children and a couple of nannies. She spent an average of two hours a day with her kids and never had dinner with them. She was more devoted to what she called "me" time: shopping, lunching, exercising, and grooming. Ah yes, the joys of motherhood!

- I was at a moving sale in a luxurious Beverly Hills villa. While I was negotiating the price of a carton of books, the owner's twelve-year-old son interrupted the conversation to sneer at me, "What difference does ten bucks make?" I decided to pass on the books, and I stole a Hot Wheels toy on the way out, to donate to a thrift shop. It was priced at two dollars, and I figured if the obnoxious rich kid despised me for caring about ten dollars, then what difference would two bucks make to him?

- On the other hand, I know some trust-fund kids who live sensibly, work hard, and are compassionate community activists with a sense of giving back.

TUITION FREE

I tried to bring up my own child in the spirit of thriftaholism, but parents, as we all know, are pushovers. I suggested to Jono that I give him piano lessons. He agreed, but only if I paid him five dollars a session. Then he convinced us that his life was not worth living unless he could play clarinet in the school orchestra. We shelled out two hundred bucks for an instrument that he lost interest in after the first class.

Luckily, he went to public school, which saved us a lot of money to throw out on blackmail piano lessons and untouched clarinets. If you're lucky enough to live near a decent public school, it's the biggest bargain around. And even if it's not totally up to par, I think you should give it a try anyway and work to improve it.

If all the prosperous educated parents who spend $22,000 a year on kindergarten would, instead, get involved with our public education system, maybe we wouldn't be living in a country where the literacy rate is lower than Kazakhstan's.

THE PLOT THICKENS

When Jonathan was a teenager, we made it clear that he was expected to get a summer job. He tried hard but couldn't find one, so I asked my architect friend Charles to give him some office work, and I would secretly pay the salary.

Jonathan came home one day and announced that Charles was not happy with his appearance. He had been showing up for work in his usual attire of stained T-shirts and scuffed sneakers, at a company that was all about style and image. So I had to go out and buy my son a whole new wardrobe so that he could earn the paycheck that I was underwriting.

In a perfect world, every family would have a mom and dad who love each other, stay married forever, and shower their children with love and guidance. My son grew up in such a family, and he still needed therapy. I guess there's no such thing as a perfect world; you just do the best you can.

ENOUGH ALREADY!

In most cultures in the world, grown children are expected to feed, clothe, and house their elders, and in many cases it's the mother-in-law who runs the family. Sounds good to me! In our society, however, parenting seems to have become a lifetime job.

After you've raised the kid and survived the childhood injuries, the teenage psychoses, and the near-bankruptcy of tuition costs, you get all teary at a college graduation ceremony and congratulate yourself on a job well done. The offspring is launched, your life is your own again, and you can start feathering that empty nest by turning the kid's room into a ceramics studio. Think again.

Young adults face a brutal shock when they leave the warm cocoon of home and school. Finding a job and a place to live are tough challenges, especially when the economy is in the crapper. Nowadays, a lot of college grads are boomeranging right back to mama's house.

If—God forbid—I had a twenty- or thirty-something living with me, I would at least expect some help with the chores. My friend Nancy is a university professor. Her son and daughter-in-law live with her. The daughter-in-law loves to cook, bake, and garden, which sounds like a pretty fair exchange to me. On the other hand, I heard of a woman who prepares her slacker son's lunch before she leaves for work and does his laundry on weekends. Someone should call the parent abuse hotline.

WHAT I DID FOR LOVE

We ran out of money just around the time that Jonathan graduated from college, so he knew he would have to make it on his own. This turned out to be the best thing that ever happened to him. He struggled for a few years and shared expenses with a few roommates. He tried a variety of jobs in film, photography, carpentry, even waiting tables when he got really desperate. Finally, I said, "What kind of job do you think would make you happiest?"

He said he'd love to work in publishing—a notoriously low-paying profession. I did not advise him to go for the money. Instead, I encouraged him to follow his dream. He got a low-level job at a dot.com that was just starting to produce audio books on the Internet. The company, Audible.com, took off, and Jono ended up being head of a department with a good salary, stock options, interesting travel, and all the other perks that I'm told people with real jobs enjoy.

Eventually, Jonathan got tired of the corporate grind and decided to take a lower paying, less stressful job at a nonprofit do-goody institution. Again, I encouraged him to follow his heart and not use "Show me the money!" as his only mantra, a relaxed, meaningful lifestyle also counts for something. Of course, I may regret this high-mindedness when I'm in my dotage and Jonathan can't afford to take care of me. Them's the chances you take.

THE BIG E

If we want our kids to have secure financial futures, we have to pay the price of educating them. The more nerdy they are as teenagers, the more successful they'll be later on. Brains earn bucks, and nobody knows this better than poor immigrants. I grew up in a neighborhood of hard-working refugees whose children all went to college, whereas I know more than one wealthy family where the kids are high school dropouts.

Judy directed my two solo shows. She has three siblings, and they grew up in blue-collar East Los Angeles. Judy's mother made sure that all the kids got music lessons, plus dance classes for the girls, even though money was scarce. When her husband complained that these classes were taking money out of the food budget, she would say, "With these lessons, when they grow up, they'll never be hungry!" And she was right: They all ended up with prosperous careers in the arts.

Years later, Judy's brother was playing trumpet in the orchestra of a Broadway show. Mama, who had never been on a plane before, traveled to New York for the opening. During the overture, her son had a solo, and she broke into enthusiastic applause. When the audience shushed her, she explained "I'm sorry, but that trumpet player was my son!" One hard-bitten New Yorker commented, "Yeah. We figured."

There are cheapo ways to enrich your kids' cultural life. I know a few families who reserve Fridays for Classic Movie Night. They make a batch of popcorn and watch old musicals, Hitchcock thrillers, and, as the kids get older, foreign masterpieces from Ingmar Bergman and Kurosawa. Dare I say an evening like this might be a better investment in your child's future than Friday night football?

But we can't do all the educating ourselves, no matter what those wacky home-schoolers think, and college costs money. As with everything else, there are always ways to save.

- Financial aid is available. Loans vary from state to state, sometimes even county to county, and the stimulus package is releasing additional federal funds for educational grants and loans.

- There are all kinds of private scholarships. Many are based on ethnicity and gender, including transgender. Some scholarships often go unused because they are so obscure and unusual, like the ones for grandchildren of World War II vets from certain platoons. Some other little-known listings I just came across include National Marbles Tournament Scholarships, the Patrick Kerr Skateboard Scholarship, and my personal favorite, the National Candy Technologists Scholarship.

- Some employers give tuition aid. I heard of a psychiatrist on staff at a New York hospital who had not only his son's college education paid for but also his private high school.

- Unions can be a source of financial help.

- I was surprised to learn that you can actually negotiate when a school offers a scholarship. If you've received a better offer from another college, you can use that as a bargaining tool, and they will often match the competition.

- There are all kinds of work–study programs, where you earn money and might actually learn something of value. My son was put to work in the college computer lab, where he acquired many useful skills. He's still the one I call when my laptop acts up.

- If your kid attends a local community college for two years, he or she can then transfer to a four-year school, and you have saved a bundle. You save on tuition, and the student can stay at home so you don't have to cover additional living expenses. Also, you can monitor the beer bingeing. Let's face it: College dorms, frat houses, and off-campus housing are cesspools of alcohol and drug excess. (Maybe the best way to guard against those dangerous experiments is to let kids have a little wine mixed with water at special occasions when they're growing up, as the French and Italians do, giving them an early lesson in moderation.)

- I spoke to Dr. Leon Botstein, president of my alma mater, Bard College, who advised, "If you want to go to college on the cheap, be a straight-A student. There is a lack of excellence in American high school students, and high achievers are greatly in demand. Your education will be paid for if you are outstanding—not only in academics but in music, science, and sports. The wealthy do not live up to their privilege, and too many affluent children are poor students." (That's because they're out with Mom at the mall, buying pricey designer outfits when they should be at home conjugating French verbs. "*J'accuse!*")

Textbook prices are insane. Students could easily pay close to $500 a semester on books they will probably never need again, like a $150 Introduction to Statistics text. You can find a lot of this stuff online, buy them used on campus, or, if possible, buddy up with a classmate.

College students are on their way to being adults, but they're not quite there yet, so we still have to deal with their juvenile choices. At the end of his sophomore year, my son announced that he had been in school all his life and was tired of it. He wanted to take a year off and get a job. I explained that this would be a lose–lose situation.

He would move back home and, if he was lucky, get some tedious menial job. He'd have a lonely, miserable time and then be a year behind his friends at school. And we would have to share our home with a depressed nineteen-year-old. No thanks.

Or he would find a good job, or meet a girl, and never go back to school. Also no thanks.

A CAUTIONARY TALE

Being a parent sometimes means saying no. And sometimes saying no costs us extra. My son announced he was going to Vegas for the weekend with some friends.

"Really? And how, may I ask, are you getting there?"

"In Dave's car; it's right outside."

I look at Dave's car, and I see death. Dave's car is an open jeep: no roof, no sides.

"If you take that car through the desert, not only will you be burned to a crisp, but you won't have any protection in a collision. Why don't you rent a nice four-door sedan?"

"We can't afford it."

"Well, here's some money. Rent a real car."

So the boys are driving back from Vegas. There's a van in front of them with a heavy glass door strapped to the roof. Suddenly this glass door comes loose, flies through the air, and crashes right on top of the boys' car! But the heavy steel roof protects the kids, and nobody gets hurt. Just doing my job, folks, just doing my job.

PARTY TIME

Coming-of-age rituals are a part of growing up: christenings, communions, sweet sixteens, *Quinceañeras*, debutante balls, whatever. They can all take a bite out of your wallet. But, thrifty as we are, that is not the main reason we did not give our son, Jonathan, a traditional bar mitzvah.

Hebrew is a sung language when it's used for prayer, and Jono can't carry a tune. I didn't want him to go through the humiliation of having to sing in public. More importantly, since we're not religious, we felt it would be hypocritical to join a temple just for this one occasion.

But we did want our son to have some kind of "now-I-am-a-man" ceremony, so we created our own secular event. We sent him to a Yiddish poet for lessons in Jewish history, culture, and literature. We invited a bunch of people over for a big lunch, and Jonathan read a speech he had written called "Jewish Values in the Modern World." Also, I had asked each guest to give Jono a list of their ten favorite books and movies so that he could have his own personal liberal arts guide.

The celebration was a huge success, and everyone congratulated us on being innovative and creative and true to our own values. Everyone, that is, except our son. He felt cheated and accused us of doing a cheapo hippy-dippy version of what could have been a much more profitable opportunity for him.

"Why didn't I have a real bar mitzvah with a party in a fancy restaurant? I would have gotten lots of money and cool gifts instead of books, pens, and those stupid lists!"

And then I remembered the first law of parenthood: Whatever choice you make, your child will resent you for it, so you might as well do what feels right to you. I told Jonathan that if he really wanted a traditional bar mitzvah with an extravagant party he would have to wait until he could pay for it himself, like Kirk Douglas did at the age of eighty-three (Mazel tov, Spartacus!) As it happens, Jono now gets a lot of pleasure and pride out of being well educated. And he admits that those "stupid lists" stirred the beginnings of his intellectual curiosity.

Word got out about our event, and a writer called to interview me. He was doing a book about people who create their own rituals. I asked to hear some of the other stories, and my favorite was about an Italian family. For many generations they have been carpenters, old-fashioned craftsmen who still carve furniture the traditional way. This is a dying art, like so many artisanal crafts. As a matter of fact, modern-day Italy has a surplus of doctors and a shortage of shoemakers. But this particular family wanted to keep their craft alive, so they had a rule: No child could eat with the grown-ups until he made his own chair. Bravo!

It's a Gift

I hate gifts. I hate giving them. I hate getting them. I hate watching people open them. I hate unwrapping presents and having to pretend that I like them. "Wow! A vegan cookbook! I've been wanting one of these!" Not only do I not want *any* kind of cookbook, but all our available shelves are crammed with Benni's volumes. This little baby is going right back to Barnes & Noble to be exchanged for something useful, like a Bette Midler CD, which I will play while dining on nonvegan takeout.

I have very specific tastes, and I'm much happier picking out my own presents. After many years of hearing "Is this some kind of a joke?" when I open his gifts (like a toaster for Valentine's Day), my poor husband has learned that the safest thing is to just take me out to dinner. Most of my friends also respect my preference for events over things wrapped in boxes, so around my birthday I get a bunch of dinner invitations that stretch the celebration out to a couple of weeks. What could be better?

A present I always do appreciate is a houseplant. Some people say, "You can't be too rich or too thin." I say, "You can't have too many flowering cymbidiums." I live in Los Angeles, where plants are cheap. I was staying with my friend Sheila in New York and went to a florist to buy her a house gift. The potted orchid that I can get in L.A. for twenty-five dollars was sixty bucks. When I pointed out the price difference, the florist explained that the plant, like me, had also flown in from California, and I was paying its airfare. As with food, I guess it's best to buy plants local.

One of the loveliest and most original gifts I've ever gotten was a birthday present from my friend Rowena. She paid in advance at my local florist for four lavish bouquets that I could order at any time during the year. How luxurious to be able to just walk around the corner at Thanksgiving and get a prepaid centerpiece!

Since I rarely keep presents, I do a lot of re-gifting. This can be a slippery slope. I once just barely averted disaster when I realized that the scented candles I was bringing as a hostess present had been given to me by the same hostess. I had just enough time to buy a box of fancy chocolates. As it turned out, my friend was on a diet and couldn't keep sweets in the house. Her guests ate some, then she insisted that I take the rest home. I guess you could call that *de*-gifting.

DO IT YOURSELF

If you're so inclined, you can show some originality with a hand-crafted present.

- Benni went to one of those pay-by-the-hour pottery studios and made a beautiful bowl for his partner's wedding gift.

- My friend Kim made me two stunning bracelets out of vintage rhinestone and Bakelite buttons. These one-of-a-kind pieces are real attention getters, and I like attention.

- One Christmas, Kim and her sister made spectacular wreaths out of twigs, pine cones, dried flowers, berries, and ribbons for all their friends. When I think of the long hours of patient labor that went into this project, I get overwhelmed with fatigue. Fortunately, not all of my friends are as indolent as I am.

- My friend Brenda picks up small ceramic containers at yard sales. When she needs to bring a house gift, she takes a cutting from one of her succulents, plants it in one of these pots, then tops it with a decorative pebble mulch.

I buy low-priced treasures whenever I find them, then wait for the right occasion. Eventually someone will appreciate that midcentury fondue set. Also, I don't always wait for a special occasion to give someone a present. Kim's mother, Ann, collects bug jewelry, so if I spot a bumblebee brooch or a ladybug pin at a yard sale, I grab it and pass it on to her. Josi, one of Benni's producing partners, has a passion for copper cookware, so I pick up pots for him, but he gets to do the polishing himself.

As icky as gift giving and gift getting can be, there's nothing ickier than *un*-gifting. Jerry, a friend from high school, married a woman whose father was in the lighting business. Jerry's father-in-law furnished every room of the newlyweds' house with lamps and sconces. A few years later, Jerry's wife left him for his best friend, and then her father showed up to take back all the lighting, leaving wifeless Jerry in the dark. Talk about cruel and unusual punishment!

POOR CHOICES

A few years ago, we were at an art fair and fell in love with the work of a fine art photographer. We splurged and bought three pieces, had them framed, and gave them as Christmas gifts—a very extravagant gesture for two cheapies like us.

What I learned from this experience was to *never ever* give art as a present. It's much too personal an item, and people's tastes vary. They all hated the photographs. Nobody actually told us this, but I have searched every wall of every room of my friends' homes, and the photographs are nowhere to be seen. One day I'll probably come across them in a thrift shop, at which point I'll buy them back, hang them up, and embarrass our friends when they visit.

The worst gift-giving disaster I've ever witnessed took place at a country wedding. Two guests drove up in a rusty old van, which turned out to be their present. The well-meaning guests assured the bridal pair that in spite of its grungy appearance, the van was in excellent running order. This turned out to be true as long as the owner had a degree in auto mechanics, since there was a need for constant repairs. The unwanted vehicle uglified the driveway for many months, until the newlyweds finally managed to give it away to a local handyman.

I would like to warn against a dangerous new trend: elaborate graduation parties for each grade of school. I've seen families in restaurants with presents and balloons honoring fifth graders. That's a little too much positive reinforcement for such a mundane accomplishment. I agree with President Obama that some things should just be taken for granted—like completing fifth grade. Let's hold off on the gift giving 'til the kid completes law school.

TYING THE KNOT

Being a wedding guest is a real challenge to the thriftaholic. It's getting out of hand when the least expensive gift on the registry is $200, and even I don't have the guts to give a yard sale item. I attended one event where all I could afford on the list was one flat sheet for $125. I made up for it by drinking extra glasses of champagne at the reception and taking home a centerpiece.

Of course, I should have remembered that, like museum admissions, the registry is only a suggestion. You can still use your imagination and give something meaningful that won't break the bank. When Jonathan got married, my artist friend Rachel invited him and his bride, Alisa, to come to her studio and select a painting. The kids were much happier with an original work of art than a set of bath towels.

I know one young woman from a prosperous family who married a guy whose folks were of modest means. She didn't want to embarrass them, so she registered at Target. I applaud her sensitivity. I wonder if you can register at The Ninety-Nine Cent Store.

When Jonathan got married, one of my friends, who has a healthy income, won the cheapskate prize with the stingiest gift: a twenty-five dollar item. I had a brief moment of resentment, but then I remembered the many acts of kindness this guy had performed over the years, including volunteering to give blood when I had a medical emergency. On the other hand, the kids got pricey presents from people who had been sorely neglectful in other ways. The cost of a gift doesn't always reflect the generosity of the giver. That's my Zen thought for the day.

My friend Susanna is an artist, and her husband, Charles, is an architect, so they have very specific taste when it comes to interior design. Unfortunately, they got married in the days before gift registries and received a set of dishes from some close relatives. The dishes were muddy brown with a yellow floral pattern, and Susanna says that any food she served looked rotten as soon as it hit the plate. Since the relatives were frequent guests, Susanna felt obligated to use the loathsome dishes. She lost a lot of weight in those years.

PRE-WEDDING PRESENTS

As if wedding gift pressure weren't bad enough, women also have to deal with the bridal shower. I was invited to such an event for the daughter of a friend. I barely knew the girl, and I was forced to sit with thirty strangers for three long hours as the bride unwrapped an endless succession of ice cream makers and waffle irons. The excitement of that wears off after a while. At the bachelor party, the guys get to drink beers and watch a stripper. Sounds like more fun to me.

In contrast, I've known and adored Kim's daughter, Molly, since she was a baby. Molly didn't want the usual gift-bash; she just wanted to spend a pleasant afternoon with a few women she felt close to.

I think it's time to rethink a lot of wedding traditions. Benni's old school chum Werner had a daughter who got engaged to a much older man. As a matter of fact, the groom was about the same age as Werner and quite a bit richer, but he still expected his in-laws to pay for the wedding.

In olden days, women were valued less than men, so the bride's family had to fork over cash, feather beds, cattle, and so on as a wedding payment. In modern times, I think the person who pays for the event should be the person with the most cattle.

We met at a botanical garden, took a lovely springtime walk, and ended the afternoon with a lavish tea.

Molly had asked that we not bring presents, but I wasn't brought up to arrive empty handed. When I was growing up in the Bronx, if you saw someone walking in the street with a pink box from the bakery, chances are that they were on their way to pay a visit. (I love that moment in *Bananas* when Woody Allen brings a cake to the dictator's mansion.)

I gave Molly a little basketful of vintage white lace and embroidered handkerchiefs for all the women in her wedding party. I had probably paid a quarter each at estate sales, but I had washed, bleached, and ironed each one with loving care. It was a personal and unusual gift, very enthusiastically received. Then again, Molly is an accomplished actress. Maybe she'd really rather carry Kleenex. Oh well, she can always re-gift the hankies.

NOT-SO-HOLY NIGHT

Christmas has gotten out of control: so much pressure, so much excess, and so much greedy materialism on a holiday that's supposed to be spiritual. And it begins earlier every year: They start playing carols in the stores shortly after Labor Day.

I think extravagant Christmas presents should be for kids— a bike, a guitar, a villa in Tuscany, whatever—and anyone over the age of twenty-one should play five-buck Secret Santa or those gift exchange games, which can be a lot of fun.

I'm not a *total* Scrooge. For one thing, I do love those twinkling lights on the darkest days of winter. One tradition that we share with friends is a nighttime walk along the Venice canals in Los Angeles. It's a quiet, traffic-free zone, with quaint little bridges, duck-filled water-ways, and charming homes illuminated with colorful holiday lights. It's an enjoyable holiday experience that doesn't cost a dime until we pig out at the local Thai restaurant. Most communities have a similar area that's especially fun to stroll through during the festive season. My real dream is to take my Christmas walk in Sicily.

THE GIFT OF GIVING

For the past few years, I've used Christmas as the time to give modest charitable donations to various organizations. And then I decided to simply give one meaningful gift to one needy person: I pay twenty-three dollars a month to PlanUSA to sponsor an eleven-year-old girl in a poor African village. That money makes it possible for her go to school.

The Talmud says that if you save one life, you save the world. I'm not exactly sure how that works, but I will happily accept the title of world saver. (I wish I could help keep a poor American kid in school, but that would cost a bit more than twenty-three bucks a month.)

I still give to certain other nonprofits, like PBS, but that's a little self-serving: I couldn't live without *Masterpiece Theatre*.

Every year we attend a huge Christmas party, and the guests are always asked to bring toys, which are then given to charity. This past year, we did not give toys; instead, we were asked to contribute to Heifer.org, which does a lot of good work in undeveloped countries.

I heard about a couple who asked for similar donations, instead of presents, for their fiftieth anniversary celebration. The next year they went to China to visit the village they had helped. I am a sloppy, sentimental sucker for stories like this; they are refreshing antidotes to all the evilness in the daily news.

Less Is More

TOO MANY WORDS

Wasting time is just as objectionable to me as wasting money. My mantra is KISS: Keep It Simple, Stupid. And not just simple, but short. My favorite joke has two words: "Pretentious? *Moi*?"

It's hard for me to sit through productions of Eugene O'Neill or August Wilson. I just don't have the patience for all the yada yada yada. A lady sitting in front of me during *Anna Christie* whispered to her neighbor, "It's a good play, but he should have had an editor." My sentiments exactly. The great theater director George Abbott said, "Remember, what you cut can't fail."

I've tried to read Proust many times, but it's a hopeless cause. My friend Pam actually owns a Proust letter. She once passed it around the dining table, which got me nervous until I realized the paper we were handling with our greasy fingers was a copy; the original was in a bank vault. The letter was three pages long, and it consisted of one sentence. I rest my case.

I canceled my subscription to *The New Yorker* after they ran that controversial cover of Barack and Michelle Obama as Muslim terrorists. I didn't believe the drawing was deliberately racist, just badly executed. A publication famous for its biting humor should not feature a cartoon whose meaning was so unclear. Once I stopped getting the magazine, I realized that I was free of having to plow through thirteen-page articles on strawberry farming. I did miss the cartoons and reviews, however, so now I just get used issues from my friends. Since I haven't paid for them, I don't feel guilty about skipping the strawberry articles.

I know a guy who, like me, does autobiographical theater pieces. I have two shows, but he has five or six. He is a witty and engaging performer, but he finds every detail of his existence so important that each show covers just one decade. They have titles like *One to Ten: The Early Years.* I call that too much information.

I sometimes coach people in public speaking as an act of self-defense: I know nothing worse than being a captive audience while someone drones on and on and on. At one wedding, the father of the bride named every single person in their family, both living and dead. This took twenty minutes, during which time I fantasized about every method I would like to use to slowly and painfully kill him.

DOUBLE-DUTY

Besides my attention deficit disorder, another reason I like things to be short and simple is an economic one: In a freelance frugalista lifestyle, time is money, so I am a compulsive multitasker.

- While I'm on hold in voicemail hell, I put the phone on speaker so I can do something constructive on the computer, like play a game of Web Boggle. If I'm feeling more industrious, I might actually write a paragraph. If I'm on hold with the cable company, I might actually write a whole book.

- I always keep a magazine on my desk, in case my psychotic computer decides to go into slo-mo. That way, I can read a restaurant review while waiting to be connected to the Net.

- If I'm eating alone, I always read something. This can be dangerous: If the book holds my attention, I will just keep stuffing my face until I find out who the murderer was.

- I play Tetris on my Game Boy while I watch *The View*.

- If I have to sew a button, I do it while listening to *This American Life*.

- When I do my morning workout, I always exercise two muscles at once, like lifting weights while doing side kicks.

- I am such a champion multitasker, I've even been known to fart while sneezing.

Transportation

WALK THE WALK

When I watch those Jane Austen series on *Masterpiece Theatre*, I'm always impressed by how much walking everyone does. They stroll to the village, they saunter to the squire's mansion, they meander through country lanes just for the simple pleasure of moving one foot in front of the other. I've always felt that Jane Austen and I were soulmates, and this proves it. I find walking is the cheapest, healthiest, pleasantest way to get from one place to the next.

Surprise fact: New Yorkers live longer than anyone in the country. You would think that the pollution, the stress, the noise of the Big Apple might not make it the healthiest place in America, but you would think wrong. Apparently, the reason for this longevity is that New Yorkers walk. They walk fast. And they carry things while they walk. I'm based in Los Angeles now, and I've noticed that when I spend a few weeks in Manhattan, I eat everything in sight (you can't get sesame noodles or a decent pumpernickel in L.A.) and always lose a few pounds.

New Yorkers are the fastest pedestrians in the country. I once arrived at Kennedy on a flight from Houston. As I sprinted off the plane, one ambling tourist drawled, "These New Yorkers are always in such a hurry!" I didn't explain to her that it's because we have something interesting to hurry *to*. I was in too much of a rush.

Lecco, a town in Italy, turned its school bus system into a walking system. The kids who had previously been driven to school now follow the same route on foot, accompanied by paid staffers and parental volunteers. This Pied Piper arrangement decreased traffic, cut down greenhouse gas emissions, and reduced childhood obesity—a win–win–win situation.

GOING PUBLIC

I won't say subways are fun, but they're faster and cheaper than cars or cabs. And I love buses, because you can view the fascinating panorama of city life as you roll by. I love buses a little less these days because of the noxious cell phone chatter. "I'm on the bus. I'll be home in five minutes." If you'll be home in five minutes, why disturb the peace by calling?

DOOR TO DOOR

Taxis and limos are expensive for just one trip, but most limo companies offer town car service. You pay an hourly rate of around forty-five bucks for a three-hour minimum. That means that four tourists in Seattle could make stops at the Space Needle, the glass and steel library, the market where they throw salmon through the air, and so on, for less than it would cost to take a cab each time, and you're traveling in style.

GENERAL MOTORING

When I moved to California, I had to adjust to car culture. I never really succeeded. I hate the constant traffic jams, I hate the smog caused by gasoline, and I hate the isolation of sitting alone in a metal box surrounded by millions of people sitting alone in *their* metal boxes. I also hate the fact that I'm the world's worst driver, and it still takes me twenty nervous, sweaty ins-and-outs to back into a parking space.

Because of my car aversion, we live in one of the few urban enclaves in the vast suburban sprawl of Los Angeles. We can walk to shops, restaurants, and theaters, while my overweight neighbors (native Californians) drive five blocks to the movies and then complain about the price of gas and parking.

The average price of a new car in the United States is $28,400, and as soon as you drive it off the lot you've already lost a bundle. We buy only used Volvo station wagons. They're safe, they last forever, and they don't cost very much. Plus they can haul a lot of yard sale junk.

Here's how it breaks down. We buy the wagon for $6,500 and keep it for two years. Then we sell it for $3,000. That means we have had a good-quality vehicle for $3,500. Of course, there are always repairs, but we're still way ahead of the game.

In New England, a Volvo station wagon is a symbol of upper middle-class prosperity. In Los Angeles, it is a zero-image ride: This is the land of Beamer convertibles. Call me shallow, but I'm ashamed to admit that if we're attending a really glamorous event I'm sometimes tempted to park a block away.

By the way, if your idea of a status car is a gas-guzzling, terrorist-funding, space-hogging SUV with a dangerous tendency to roll over, my only tip for you is to have your head examined.

Suren started out as Benni's intern and now is his co-producer. He bought an almost-new Prius on eBay at a big savings, and he didn't have to be wait-listed for six months. The owner was located in Chicago, where Suren's mom lives, so she picked up the car and drove it out to her son in L.A. That's what mothers are for.

Here's a surprising fact about hybrids: They cut down on gas usage, but if you're seriously trying to reduce your carbon footprint it is more Earth-friendly to buy a used car of any brand. It takes a heap of energy to build a new vehicle, even a green one.

And here's a clever concept. You can be car free by joining Zipcar, a car-sharing company. You just reserve a car whenever you need one and pay by the hour. Gas and insurance are included.

I'm all for carpooling. Whether you're driving to the office or dropping the kids off at school, it makes sense to share the fuel costs while reducing road congestion. This might force you to miss your favorite NPR shows, but you can hear them later online.

There are lots of senior transportation programs all over the country. They provide taxi vouchers, group vans, and volunteer drivers to help older people get to stores and medical appointments. I hate to sound ageist, but this is a much better idea than having ninety-year-olds behind the wheel. My Danish mother-in-law drove herself to her country house every week, long after she could barely see or hear.

TWO-WHEELERS

In many European countries, bicycles are the most popular way of getting around. This is a good thing. Like walking, cycling is cheap, healthful, and environmentally sound. Enlightened cities like Copenhagen, Paris, and Amsterdam offer free communal bikes in order to cut down on car traffic. Bicycle culture isn't for every city, though; it might not be too practical in San Francisco. Otherwise, it sounds like a great idea to me, if I only knew how to ride a bike.

Getting Help
from the Pros

PART

IV

Gyms: Are They Really Necessary?

WORK IT!

Exercise is a way of life for many Americans. Whether it's Curves, Swerves, or Yoga Booty Ballet, we like to get out there and make our muscles tough and buff. I used to love dance classes—jazz, tap, modern. Actually, that's a lie. I did not love modern. That class was a little too airy-fairy for me. When the instructor said, "Now turn yourself into a flower blossom and float over to your neighbor's garden," this little blossom just floated right out of the studio and never went back.

Benni and I took some ballroom dancing courses. We learned swing, foxtrot, and some rumba but never worked our way up to salsa. That's still on my to-do list.

I've also enjoyed yoga classes: the serene atmosphere, the gentle spinal stretches, and the soothing chants. During the guided relaxation, for the first time in my life I was able to reach a true meditative state—if snoring with your mouth open while spittle runs down your chin can be called a true meditative state.

Yoga can also save you money on medical bills. When we got married, Benni had chronic lower-back problems. Every few months he went into spasm, could barely walk, couldn't lift anything, and—dare I say it?—was not too much fun in the sack. He saw acupuncturists, chiropractors, and finally an orthopedist who scheduled him for an operation, confirming the old adage, "Ask a surgeon a question and you'll get a cutting reply."

Spinal surgery seemed like a radical and expensive solution, so I convinced Benni to try yoga. He felt immediate relief and canceled the surgery. He has done yoga stretches every day of his life ever since and has never once had a recurrence of back pain. This was over forty years ago.

We've also dabbled in tai chi but never made much progress. The difference between the positions was a little too subtle for me: I was never sure if I was doing Repulse Monkey or Snake Creeps Down.

I no longer go to any of these classes for two reasons: You have to leave home to get there, and they cost money.

When we lived in New York, the yoga studio was across the street. Now, in Los Angeles, the teacher I like is thirty-five minutes away, and I'm the world's most frazzled driver. The soothing effects of the class will be gone by the time I have completed the nerve-wracking ride home.

Also, classes and gym memberships are expensive, so now I work out at home. It's cheaper than a gym, plus I don't have to be exposed to all those size-two twenty-somethings jabbering about the latest fad diet. I picked up a mat and some weights, and I start every day by doing one of the many workout tapes I buy at yard sales for fifty cents. I've got everything from *10-Minute Abs* to vintage Jane Fonda and Richard Simmons videos. To vary my routine, I also have a few yoga DVDs.

You can also get free workouts on the Net, like Spark People, Exercise TV, and Yoga Journal, just to name a few. (On many of these sites, you have to tolerate the hyper-perky language, like "Six-Minute Butt Blaster!") My next project will be to try the flamenco dance classes at Expert Village. I am charmed by the instructor's accent: "Bend your neeze a leetle beet."

Another plus of exercising at home is that I know my body, so no one can force me to do moves that might be harmful. My friend Tony paid a lot to join a "boot camp" that met in a public park every morning. The teacher was as demanding as a drill sergeant—and about as compassionate—and a lot of people in the group ended up with long-term, costly injuries. No thanks.

Why buy a treadmill when you can just speed-walk around the neighborhood? My friend Rowena joins me twice a week for half an hour. We carry weights and gossip breathlessly while keeping up a vigorous pace—another fine example of multitasking.

The Shop Around the Corner: $2 Local Merchants

I had an ink stain on a silk cocktail dress. My fancy neighborhood cleaner wanted twenty dollars, with no guarantee that the stain would come out. I had paid only two bucks for the dress at a rummage sale, so I decided to shop around. I tried another local place, and they assured me ink stains are impossible to remove.

I left my neighborhood and went to a dry cleaner in a less yuppified area. They removed the stain on the spot and charged me eight bucks. I also discovered that their tailor charges half of what I pay at my local seamstress. Location, location, location.

We have found this same location rule to be true of auto mechanics: Prices are lower in blue-collar neighborhoods, and the quality of the work can be excellent. Of course, it takes a little time to get there, and I sometimes succumb to laziness and pay extra for the convenience of nearby shops.

SERVICE CALLS

I do stay local when it comes to household services like heating and plumbing: The big chains charge a lot more than small independent companies. I needed to replace the locks on two doors. The large chain would have charged forty-five dollars for the visit, plus eighty-six dollars for each lock. The local guy came for thirty-five dollars, plus sixty-four dollars for the locks.

I will admit I got a little nervous when the neighborhood electrician arrived. He was so old and frail that I had to help him up the front steps. Then he forgot a tool in his van, so I had to help him down the front steps and back up again. Fortunately, he was not charging by the hour, and he ended up doing a swell job. This was no surprise, as he had ninety years of experience.

Technophobia

I am so technically challenged that when something goes wrong with my laptop, I can't even call for help because the technicians always have questions that I am too dumb to answer. They said, "How do you get your Internet?" The correct answer would have been, "Time Warner cable." My reply was, "Uh, it's in my computer and I just click onto it." And it's not just the computer that mystifies me; it's the digital camera, the cell phone, the Palm Pilot, the DVD player, and the TiVo system. The only modern device I can operate without assistance is my electric toothbrush.

I realized a few years ago that I would have to find a part-time-once-in-a-while techie nerd who would be patient with my ignorance and not charge a fortune. In many homes that person would be the resident twelve-year-old, but our nest is empty, so I called the Geek Squad and asked their prices. They don't have an hourly rate; they charge a flat fee for each specific job. Hooking up a printer, for example, costs $150. I don't think so.

Then I looked at some online ads for home tech help. The hourly rate averaged between sixty and ninety bucks. Since that's more than I earn, I decided to find my own private geek. I took a free ad on Craigslist and offered twenty bucks an hour, figuring I would get a high school student. I got so many responses from overqualified adults that I had to remove the ad after half a day—and this was *before* the country went into the Second Great Depression. Some responders were retirees who wanted a little extra cash. Some were graduate students. Some seemed highly qualified but had accents that were just too difficult to decipher.

A few friends expressed concern about my letting a stranger into the house, but I interviewed all the applicants over the phone and felt confident that I could weed out the crazies—like the guy who laughed maniacally at everything I said. I finally settled on Jay, a young filmmaker who was between gigs. I felt guilty about paying him so little, so I promised to find him other clients who could pay more. This took only a few phone calls to the Yenta Brigade: Everyone I know needs tech help.

The first thing Jay helped me with was my TiVo problem. I had an old unit that had become very unreliable, and there's nothing more tragic than sitting down with some tea and cookies to watch the latest installment of *Lost* and discovering that you have recorded one hour of the Shopping Network.

Jay happened to have an extra unused unit, which he sold me for a hundred bucks, and he installed it for me. Then he spent two hours on the phone with someone in the Philippines, trying to figure out why the new unit was as erratic as the old one. It turned out to be a problem with the phone line, so he got us a little gizmo that connects the TiVo to our cable system. A nice little bonus was that he convinced them to continue my original free lifetime contract. I could never, ever, in a million years have accomplished any of this myself.

Then Jay installed a program in my computer called Crossloop, which allows him to log on to my computer from his home when I have a problem. It saves him travel time, and it saves me from having to get out of my pajamas, which I often don't do until 4 P.M.

It turned out that Jay also likes to do handyman work, so he has fixed a broken gate and installed some security lights. I wonder if he could cut Benni's hair.

Jay turned me on to two Web sites that offer great deals

on electronics: www.fatwallet.com and www.microsoft-

livesearch.com.

Beauty Business

LET'S MAKE UP

When it comes to cosmetics, as in so many other things, costlier ain't necessarily better. Drugstore L'Oreal skin care products are cheaper than department store Lancôme, but they are made by the same company, and the formulas are pretty much identical.

I spoke to professional makeup artist Maura Knowles, who agreed that buying in the drugstore is like getting the generic brand rather than the pricey label for pretty much the same product. She assured me that the pros use a lot of drugstore items, like Maybelline mascara.

Of course, you get better service in department stores. I particularly love those free makeovers. In theory, there are no strings attached, but I always feel obliged to buy a little something after someone has been working on my face for half an hour. I guess that's why I own five unopened MAC blushers.

At flea markets in New York, there's always a booth with cosmetics at rock-bottom prices. Many of the items are the samples that come in free gift offers. I load up whenever I'm in town. Occasionally I'll come home and discover that a lipstick has dried out, but since I bought five of them at a dollar a pop, and they retail for fourteen bucks, I'm still ahead of the game.

KISS MY FACE

I treat myself to a facial every few months. Since I'm a lazy-ass who sometimes goes to bed without removing my makeup, I figure I'd better get my grubby old pores thoroughly cleaned out once in a while.

The best cosmetologists seem to come from Eastern Europe, where beauty and grooming are part of the cultural tradition: Remember the Gabor sisters? So I always look for someone named Olga or Magda. I find them by word of mouth since these small neighborhood services do not advertise or have Web sites. As a matter of fact, the women barely speak English, but they know what they're doing.

There's soft music playing, and while I lie in a semi-snoozy state the facialist steams, cleans, plucks, waxes, massages, and squeezes for almost two hours. For this I pay around sixty bucks. The name-brand salons are inconveniently located, they charge about $175 for the same treatment, and they push their high-price products at you. No thanks. I'm sticking to Svetlana.

HAIR TODAY, GONE TOMORROW

I have occasionally tried celeb-type Beverly Hills hair salons and didn't think much of the experience. The parking was impossible, the tipping was awkward, and the results were less than magnificent. (I will admit that since I have short, curly hair, there's not that much magnificence possible.)

A lot of upscale salons have training nights, where you get a free haircut from a Frédéric Fekkai wannabe. I prefer finding someone affordable within walking distance, hopefully a gay man with a decent sense of style who likes to talk about movies.

For me, part of the beauty of beauty services is the personal connection. I share recipes with my Vietnamese manicurist and looked at wedding pictures of my Russian masseuse (who charges fifty bucks an hour to come to the house). I love my life.

There are beauty schools all over the country, and the students need to practice on someone—under strict supervision, of course. These are great places for really cheap services. My local school, Marinello, offers:

Haircut with blow dry $9.95

Semipermanent color $17.95

Basic facial (thirty minutes) $15.95

Basic manicure $6.95

Bikini wax (female only) $15.95

It took me a moment to consider the implications of that last one.

$5 Health Care

I was thinking of leaving this chapter as a blank page because medical costs are a real problem, and I'm not the one to solve it. However, there are a few tricks that can help ease the burden.

- The most obvious way to lower your doctor bills is to live a healthy lifestyle. That means cutting back on the booze, smokes, pork rinds, and certain—but not all—recreational drugs. It also means having a daily exercise routine and walking or biking instead of driving.

- You can go online and order your medicines from Canada. It's legal, safe, and much cheaper than buying the same items here. One southern U.S. senator objected to this practice, warning against using "socialist medicines." If you are absolutely dedicated to unregulated free-market capitalism, then I think you should stick to your guns and pay top dollar for your pills.

- Medical tourism allows you to get low-price surgery in state-of-the-art hospitals around the world. The cost is a small fraction of what it is in the States. A heart valve replacement that would cost more than $200,000 here is $10,000 in India, including round-trip airfare and a brief vacation package. And I'll bet the food is tastier than U.S. hospital fare. Anyway, the only time I was ever in a hospital I noticed that many of the physicians were Indian, so why not let them treat you on their home turf?

- I have a couple of friends who had cosmetic surgery in Costa Rica, at great savings. The clinic was in a pleasant suburban villa, and the doctor was American trained and board certified.

- Community health centers offer care on a sliding-fee basis. You can find them at www.findahealthcenter.hrsa.gov.

- You can get free cholesterol and blood pressure checks at hospital health fairs.

- My friend Penny buys her contact lenses online, at a healthy discount, and I order aspirins and vitamins on eBay.

- Most dental schools have low-cost clinics. A student will do the procedure, supervised by a professor. There's a lot of waiting around in these places, so bring a book.

Should you throw out medicine after the expiration date? Not necessarily. An expired pill won't harm you; it just won't have the full strength of the original prescription. Pills get weaker with age, just like the rest of us.

There are many mental health centers that charge for therapy on a sliding scale. At the California Counseling Center in L.A., some patients pay as little as fifteen bucks a session—sometimes less in special circumstances. I go to the annual fundraising gala for this center. I love it, because I always win something in the silent auction.

Other
People's Money

PART

V

Friends with Benefits

We all have friends who are richer than we are. Here are some thoughts on dealing with the money gap.

MIS-MANNERS

When I was a single woman in New York, my piano teacher used to invite his more advanced students for little musical soirées. One of the students was Peggy Rockefeller, and she often brought her husband, David, chairman of Chase Manhattan Bank and owner of half the world.

The dilemma for me with the Rockefellers was: How do you behave in the presence of such enormous wealth and power? I decided that I would just be myself. In my case, this is often a poor choice.

So Peggy came without David one night, and at the end of the evening I said, "Peggy, I'm going crosstown. Do you wanna split a cab?" Dumb, dumb, dumb. You do not ask a Rockefeller if she wants to split a cab. She has no idea what I'm talking about, because really rich people never use money. She finally gets it and says, "That's all right, dear. I have a car waiting. Why don't I just drop you off?"

That winter was a bitterly cold one, so I went to a thrift shop and found a vintage raccoon coat. It was snuggly warm, and I loved it, although it did have a slightly gamey odor. One night I went to a concert at Lincoln Center and I ran into Peggy, David, and several members of their family with those rich WASP names like Buffy, Muffy, Missy, and Happy. I guess Sneezy was out of town.

Peggy graciously invited me to sit with them, explaining that they had extra seats. The rest of the hall was packed, but our row, the very first one, was empty. I suspect it was always reserved for the Rockefellers. They put me on the aisle, and Peggy was down at the other end. They had done the classy thing of checking their coats, but I had my big, bulky, smelly raccoon on my lap.

Peggy, always thoughtful, leaned forward and said, "Annie, I have an empty seat next to me. Why don't you pass down your coat? You'll be more comfortable." So, much to my mortification, my stinky old fur was passed down the row from David to Buffy to Muffy to Missy to Happy to Peggy. Hanging out with society folk can have its challenging moments.

USE, BUT DON'T ABUSE

A friend complained that she went out to dinner with a wealthy acquaintance, and when the check came, the well-to-do lady suggested that they pay with two cards. My friend was offended: "She could easily have afforded to treat me." This may have been true, but if I were rich, I might resent always being expected to pick up the tab.

I have several prosperous friends who share their wealth liberally. I appreciate their generosity, but I don't want to be a freeloader. Actually, that's not quite true: I'd love to be a freeloader, but I don't want to lose my friends. For example, if someone invites me out to dinner, I check the prices on the menu and order the sixteen dollar pasta rather than the forty-two buck osso bucco.

One of my frequent hosts is from an old-money family and was brought up never to discuss the price of anything. But he did actually break down and confess how taken aback he was at one dinner guest's behavior: When the waiter took drink orders, my friend's guest said,

"I'll have a glass of your finest champagne!" That was a thirty-dollar cocktail, and then he ordered a second one. Pretty darn ballsy, if you ask me.

Years ago, I visited Benni on a film shoot in Bermuda. The executive producer invited us to dinner, and I was planning to do my usual price scanning when I received what the restaurant called "The Ladies' Menu." It had the same selections as the regular menu, but without any prices. I found this practice bizarre, but what do you expect from a place where men dine out in dinner jackets, ties, and plaid shorts?

PAYBACK

Like everyone else, wealthy people appreciate having their generosity reciprocated. Every once in a while I take some affluent friends to one of my exotic restaurants that have great food in offbeat locations, like a Oaxacan place in a mini-mall next to a 7-Eleven. This is appreciated only by folks with a sense of adventure, which leaves out one friend who will eat only in restaurants with linen napkins. I considered suggesting that she simply bring her own napkin, but didn't think she would cotton (or linen) to that idea.

Sometimes I entertain some of these rich folks at informal get-togethers at home. My friend Bob became a hot-shot Hollywood producer and spends his evenings being driven from one celeb event to another. I invited him over for a non-celeb event: a little reunion of half a dozen long-time friends. I prepared curried turkey salad, and Benni made a mountain of sweet potato pancakes. Bob's wife had warned me that even if they could come, it would only be a brief stop because they had their usual lineup of parties. They did drop by, and they enjoyed the casual fun so much that they stayed the whole evening. I think it was Benni's pancakes that did it.

I am very close to Pam, a writer who is getting on in years. She lives at the top of a Beverly Hills canyon, and we are frequent guests in her home. I used to reciprocate, but she has become frail and now needs to stay on her own turf. True, she has a housekeeper who prepares the food and does the cleanup, but I still feel obliged to offer a little payback.

So every once in a while, I bring the entire dinner. Pam is from a small town in Illinois, and although she is a brilliant and sophisticated woman, her food tastes are still stuck in the Midwest. She refers to pasta as "noodles" and once served us a green Jell-O dish that she called "salad." So we just pick up something simple, like a roast chicken with a variety of side dishes. She appreciates the effort, and so does her housekeeper.

It's a good idea to treat your rich friends' servants respectfully. I have a friend whose brother, David, is a butler for a zillionaire. One houseguest took David aside, slapped some cash into his hand, and asked him to get him some cocaine. This was not appreciated by David, or by the zillionaire when he got wind of it.

GOING DUTCH

Splitting the bill can be a slippery slope. Wealthy people don't study the prices the same way we do. If we've had risotto and salad and they've each had a dozen oysters and a 2-pound lobster, it doesn't seem quite fair to split the bill equally, and it's icky to ask for separate checks. Things get even ickier if the richies are heavy drinkers. I try to avoid sharing the tab with people who need two martinis and several glasses of wine to get through the evening. As a matter of fact, I try to avoid *being* with people who need two martinis and several glasses of wine to get through the evening.

ALMS FOR THE POOR

Besides their generous hospitality, my wealthy friends have been helpful to me in other ways. A while back, I developed my first solo show, *Yenta Unplugged.* I wrote the book, lyrics, and music. It was a total me-me-me production. (It had to be, since I'm the only person I get along with.) I had an opportunity for a theatrical production, but the producers wanted me to bring in some of the money. So I went begging. Pam allowed me to use her impressive home for a backers' audition. I invited a bunch of people, did a presentation of the show, and managed to raise the needed funds.

Theater is a risky business, and that particular run was not a successful venture, although I've done better since then. When I told Pam how awful I felt for squandering her $5,000, she said, "Not to worry. I invested as much as I was willing to lose." Sweet of her, but I still agonize over it, and I will never use friends as investors again.

Another time, we were low on cash, so Pam bought a Picasso vase from us for $3,000—with the understanding that we could buy it back at any time for the same amount. That vase is worth quite a bit more now, so maybe one day we'll take her up on that offer.

A TWO-WAY STREET

You may wonder what I've done to deserve such devotion. The answer is simple: I've tried my best to be a good and loyal friend.

As I said, Pam doesn't get out much, so I visit when I can, and I call her twice a week just to chit-chat: politics, books, gossip, whatever. Since Pam loves getting advice and I love telling people what to do, our favorite conversation begins with her saying, "Annie, I need to ask your opinion about something." This will keep us happily occupied for about an hour.

Pam writes historical novels, and I read everything before she sends it out and give her copious notes. These are big, fat books and I know nothing about the Middle Ages, so this is a time-consuming labor of love.

At one point, Pam's agent was not being very effective, and she decided to look for new representation. I hooked her up with my friend Julia, who took her on and made an immediate sale. The book did very well all over the world, and Pam was extremely grateful for the introduction, as was Julia. Some people thought I should have asked for a finder's fee. I don't agree: Friends don't charge friends for favors.

FAMILY MATTERS

Richies are wary of being loved for their dough, especially by members of their family. My friend Joy hears from her grandchildren only when they want money. She has put these kids through college and graduate school, taken them on European vacations, and paid for years of summer camps and psychotherapy.

The grandchildren have never thanked Joy for her largesse. Plus, she is a biographer, and the kids have never bothered to read any of her books. Finally, enough was enough. These days, when the kids call to say they can't pay their bills, Joy answers, "Sorry honey, the well has run dry." Maybe she's being too hard on them—perhaps she should blame her own children for their offsprings' sense of entitlement—but I don't blame her for feeling exploited.

My own son is very fond of Joy, but he lives far away and they don't have much contact, although when he comes to L.A. we usually pay her a visit. Jonathan has read Joy's books and enjoys discussing them with her. When I mentioned that he was getting married, Joy asked for his address so she could send a little gift.

That "little gift" was $1,000! When I called to say how stunned I was at her generosity, she said, "Well, Jonathan has never asked me for anything, and he's always shown interest in what I do. Also, he called immediately to thank me." I guess there's a lesson to be learned here, and the Beatles said it best in "The End." I was too cheap to pay $400 to quote the exact line, but it has to do with getting back what you give. Of course, there are other people Jonathan has been equally attentive to, and they've never given him a dime. What's their problem?

CASH COWS

I certainly appreciate the free dinners and the cash gifts, but I'm not a total whore: My wealthy friends happen to be people I genuinely care about. However, I did once meet a rich old dowager who complained that her family had abandoned her and that she was very lonely. She took a great shine to me and begged me to come and visit whenever I had the time.

In a shameful moment of greedy grubbiness, it occurred to me that if I played my cards right I could end up in her will, but I never did go see her. I just didn't find her very congenial, especially after she told me how much she admires Ann Coulter. If I had taken her up on her offer, would that have been morally reprehensible? I'm not so sure. After all, I would have been doing this friendless old woman a service. In the same vein, I hesitate to pass judgment on people who marry for money; I suspect they often earn it.

ALL IN THE TIMING

A Famous Film Director was at one of my dinner parties, and one of the guests asked him, in front of everyone, if he would consider making a donation to some struggling dance company. It put the film director (and me) in an awkward position. Wealthy people are hounded for charitable contributions every day of the week. The ones I know give generously to their own pet projects, and they should be able to swallow their food without having to fend off requests.

Also, it was my house, and my wealthy person, and that pushy guest should have understood that if Mr. Rich Guy had any extra funds for needy artists, then the first person in line should have been me. After all, I was the one who made the turkey–salsa loaf!

If you have affluent friends, you sometimes have to be protective. I've gotten many phone calls saying, "Could I have so-and-so's number? I need financing for my Native American poetry project." Or "My son needs a job. Could you get him an interview with so-and-so?" I exercise caution: Sometimes I try to help, and sometimes I feel it would be an inappropriate abuse of my friendship with Mr. Rich Guy.

Sheila lets us stay with her in her roomy Manhattan apartment when we come into town, sometimes for many weeks. She never asks for money, but we try to contribute in other ways. I take care of most of the food shopping, and Benni cleans the litter box and does small repairs. We bought her a VCR (in the days of VCRs) and have had the piano tuned and the windows washed. I once bought a bunch of plants for the terrace, but they didn't make it through a cool, windy spring. Our most appreciated gift, though, was a kitten: Sheila's first pet, Siglinda. She's been a cat lover ever since.

AFFLUENZA

I've been a guest in lavish homes with views, pools, gardens, art collections, private beaches, and all the other trappings of upscale living. They are great places to visit, but believe it or not, I wouldn't want to live there. That's because I enjoy having something to look forward to. I need those April showers that bring May flowers.

I love planning vacations: I love dreaming about sitting with a book by a landscaped pool, enjoying a spectacular view. If I had all the amenities of a luxury resort every day of my life, I suspect the thrill would wear off. That's why rich people need to enlarge their properties with stables, tennis courts, vineyards, and so on. It seems to be the human condition that whatever you've got, you always want more.

Then there's the moral question: When most people in the world don't own a book or a toilet, does a family of four really need a McMansion with six master suites and a gift-wrapping room?

Of course, major Hollywood players do need sumptuous homes for business reasons. You can't entertain 100 people at a pre-Oscar dinner in a two-bedroom condo.

Our lawyer's wife, Marcie, was decorating a new home and was frustrated: The bed linens hadn't arrived yet, which meant she couldn't buy towels. This would never be a problem for me: I am so uncouth that I had no idea that the towels must match the bedspread. I guess being rich creates its own set of problems.

I once heard two millionaires ragging each other about who had the better private jet: One was bigger, but the other had a cabin designed by a famous artist. I've since learned that private jets are environmentally irresponsible, but I'm shallow enough to regret I never got to ride on one—like, maybe, Air Force One.

THE GUEST FROM HELL

Benni's pal Dave, a trust-fund kid, occasionally invites friends to his huge family ranch in northern California. Dave is a generous host, and he is also very considerate of his staff. So he wasn't too pleased when one new-agey guest decided to replace the cook for dinner. The soy veggie burgers were not a big hit, especially with the cowhands, who rarely eat veggie anything. The cowboys were even more mystified the next day, when the inappropriate guest put on a teensy-weensy bikini and did her yoga workout on the front lawn. Dave will not be inviting this person back to the ranch any time soon.

I've hung out with many well-heeled people, but there are still things about them that baffle me.

- Why do so many rich men marry dull women?
- Why do so many rich women think it's attractive to look like they've had face transplants?
- Where do rich people hide all their electric cords?
- Why do female ballroom dancers dress like hookers?

This last has nothing to do with rich people; it's just another thing that baffles me.

Sharing the Wealth

$2

POOL CLUB

We all own a lot of stuff that we use only once in a great while. The rest of the time, it just takes up space. Do twenty families on the block really need twenty paper shredders? Why don't they all just chip in on one? Or buy a pair of scissors?

When we had a country house, I had fantasies about putting in a pool until my neighbors got one. They invited everyone on the road to come by for a swim whenever they felt like it. During the week, we had it to ourselves, and on weekends it was a pleasant gathering place to catch up on the local gossip: "That Victorian house sold for how much?" It was the cheap rural version of a suburban country club.

Now I live in Los Angeles, where there are a kazillion pools that, truth be told, rarely get used. I occasionally hear the people two houses down splashing around, but I don't know them. I've only lived on the block nine years, and L.A. is not a neighborly place. I'm trying to figure out a subtle way of putting on my swimsuit, ringing their bell, and saying, "Hi! My name is Annie. Can we be friends?"

KEEP IT CIRCULATING

Free exchange is a great way to process unwanted goods. My friend Sara lives in an upscale apartment building in Manhattan. There is an area in the lobby where tenants drop off used books and magazines for anyone to take.

I know some women who get together every few months to recycle their wardrobes. Everyone donates a bag of used clothes, and then fills up that same bag with other people's discards. I love this idea and wonder how it could be used for a variety of discarded items. How about ex-husbands?

Don't laugh! I actually have heard of singles who give "leftover parties." Each person brings someone they like, or maybe have dated in the past, but in whom they have no romantic interest. I suppose this is a legitimate form of sharing the wealth, although I don't know if I'd want to be advertised as a reject.

An actress friend and her older brother got a puppy when they were kids. They were going to have to share the pleasures and also the responsibilities of caring for this pet, but the brother set some pretty harsh terms: "I get the top half and you get the bottom." This was good training for my girlfriend who, as she puts it, "became very good at taking care of assholes." Her brother went on to become a movie mogul with a reputation for being a tough negotiator. No surprise there.

YOU DON'T HAVE TO OWN IT TO LOVE IT

My friend Susanna and her husband love dogs but can't handle the full-time responsibility of a pet. They have a pal who works long hours and hates leaving his poodle, Lulu, alone all day. So Susanna takes Lulu a few days a week and spoils her to death, and the owner picks up his tired but happy dog at the end of the day. Kind of like babysitting a grandchild.

Speaking of which, I must strongly urge every reader of this book to respect the following commandment: When you're talking to someone whose child got married recently, do *not* ask, "When are you going to be a grandmother?" I have been on the receiving end of this one for a year now, and it's very hard not to respond with, "And when are you going to grow a brain?"

Not only don't I know *when* I'm going to be a grandmother, I don't even know *if* I'm going to be a grandmother, and that's fine with me. There are plenty of children in the world; not everyone has to be a breeder. I have two nieces whose three boys are the smartest, cutest kids I know, and they seem to enjoy my company. When one of those little sweeties climbs up onto my lap, that is what I call sharing the wealth.

I met a woman who sadly described herself as childless. But then I learned that she is extremely close to her stepchildren and to various nieces and nephews. She defined herself inaccurately. I would call her "child-rich."

An acquaintance, Lena, is a single mother of three kids in Stockholm. She went back to school to get her Ph.D., and she needed help with her tough schedule. Her children were lovingly cared for on weekends by childless or retired people who enjoyed spending time with kids. These folks were volunteers in a government program that helps children in beleaguered families. We have organizations like Big Brothers and Big Sisters that have a similar goal.

Jason, one of my regular yard sale customers, is a retired Broadway dancer. He has been a Big Brother to Aaron since early childhood. When he was ten, Aaron asked his mother a delicate question: He knew Jason was gay, and he loved Jason, so did that mean that he was gay too? This turned out not to be the case, and when the boy grew up and got married, he asked Jason to choreograph the first dance. Should Jason describe himself as "childless"? I don't think so.

> Kathy, a member of my poker group, loves dogs, but no pets are allowed in her building, so she volunteers on weekends to walk dogs at the pound. There's always a way.

COME TOGETHER

You don't have to be a hippie, a polygamist, or a kibbutznik to see the advantages of extended households.

- My cousins in Connecticut live on a huge old apple orchard. The father has one house, and his son and daughter each have their own home on the property. They enjoy their togetherness but never visit without calling first.

- I know three Danish siblings who live together but separately in an elegant old villa near Copenhagen. They each have one beautiful floor-through apartment and share the garden. Once or twice a week there is a communal dinner. They all have kids, and having been an only child, I think this is an ideal way to grow up. If it takes a village, why not create a village? Of course, I might be idealizing something that could have its pitfalls. There are plenty of families who couldn't live together without murdering each other. That might not be too ideal for the kids.

- Women tend to live longer than men, and I've had many discussions with my gal pals about how to survive if we suddenly find ourselves alone. We have this fantasy of a communal home where we split the expenses, share the chores, and enjoy cultural activities—kind of like *Big Love* but without Big Daddy.

- My brother-in-law, Søren, had an apartment in a communal building in Copenhagen with a bunch of creative friends. They played music together, discussed politics, and shared state-of-the-art electronics. They also indulged in a lot of hanky-panky. Remember, this is Denmark, where hanky-panky is the national pastime.

Bartering

$3

I'LL CLEAN YOUR HOUSE
IF YOU BREASTFEED MY BABY

There are lots of ways to save money by exchanging goods and services. My friend Guillaume is a landscape designer, and he came over a few times to spruce up my garden. In return, he hauled off a heap of my extra plantings for his own backyard. I also fed him while he worked and invited him and his wife, Laura, out to dinner when the job was finished.

This was a great deal for me but not so good for Guillaume. He forgot that you have to wear lots of protection when pruning a fig tree because the sap contains an allergen similar to poison ivy. The poor guy ended up with an evil rash on both arms. He and Laura are in the process of adopting a child, so I guess I'll have to volunteer some babysitting time.

My neighbor Evelyn wanted me to coach her in public-speaking techniques and asked what I would charge. I would normally get a hundred dollars an hour, but I didn't feel comfortable asking her for money. Instead, she brought me a fully cooked dinner of chicken in wine sauce, roasted white and sweet potatoes, three different vegetable dishes, salad, home-baked bread, and a strawberry–rhubarb pie. There was enough food for three days. I've never actually gotten my $100 fee, because the people who come to me for coaching always seem to have something better than cash to offer.

My friend Tana is a documentary filmmaker who occasionally treats herself to a pricey haircut. The owner of the salon needed some photos of the shop, and Tana is a pretty good photographer, so she took some pictures for him. In return, she got some free restylings. Tana's roommate, Ann, is a computer whiz, so when Tana's laptop misbehaves, she does Ann's laundry in return for some emergency tech help.

I heard about a wine dealer who pays for his therapy with fine vintage reds. This may explain why one of my many shrinks was not always quite focused during our sessions. Those glazed eyes may have been the result of sipping the previous patient's payment.

If you like living in a house while on vacation, there are many online sites that offer home exchange listings. In Sweden and Denmark, you can actually swap apartments on a permanent basis, even if you're just a renter. Someone looking to downsize from a large suburban home might trade for a smaller place in a central location. How cool is that? Those Scandinavians are *so* civilized! Except when they drink.

There is a free market at St. Mark's Church in New York's East Village. Once a month, people swap all manner of goods and services, from clothing to free haircuts to yoga lessons. Why doesn't every church do this? And every temple, every mosque, every school, every apartment building, and every block?

You can swap things online at Swapstyle.com. I joined but didn't have the patience to figure out the system. Someone should create a Swapping for Dummies site.

TimeBanks.org creates community Web sites where local members exchange services, but not necessarily with each other. You bank your favors. Every hour that you donate earns you a Time Dollar to spend on having someone doing something for you. One member got private cooking lessons in exchange for watering a vacationing neighbor's plants. Cool!

Nickel and Diming

PART

VI

Turning Garbage into Money

Everybody owns things that are useless to them but may have value to others. I heard about someone who discovered a stash of unused Woodstock concert tickets in her mother's attic. She is getting nice prices for them on eBay.

Of course, we've all seen those thrilling moments on Antiques Road Show when someone brings in an item they've picked up for a few bucks that turns out to be worth a fortune. I always hope that the previous owner is not watching the show. "Oh look, Honey, that's Granny's ratty old Navajo blanket that we got rid of at the church sale. Fiftythousandwhat?!"

One man's garbage is another man's godsend. The old-money rich have always known this. They hold onto their stuff forever, and their possessions just keep increasing in value. Of course, the rest of us do not have the space to store our great-grandfather's first car, but I still think we are too casual about trashing stuff.

I've had a minor career as a TV actress. One day my agent sent me on an audition for a new show. The only reason I got the call was because a better-known actress refused to go, saying the part was too small. I have no pride, and I happily accepted the audition. I booked the job, which turned into the recurring character of Doris Klompus on *Seinfeld*. (I also played a second character: that obnoxious airline passenger sitting next to Elaine in economy class.)

I never considered these roles very significant, and I threw out my scripts as soon as the tapings were over. Stupid stupid stupid! Why didn't I get them all signed by the cast and Larry David, the producer? They might have been a valuable legacy for my son.

I got smarter when I did another hit show. It was a pleasant job, but I was annoyed that the pay rate was a take-it-or-leave-it, non-negotiable fraction of what I usually get. Apparently, big Hollywood studios can't afford to pay supporting actors a living wage. So I asked the star to sign my script, then went home and sold it on eBay for $300, which helped bring my earnings closer to what I should have been paid in the first place.

Some People Are Just Too Cheap

'm all for thrifty, but some folks take it a bit too far, especially some rich folks, like the wealthy woman who invited us to her penthouse apartment for lunch, handed out takeout menus, and collected our money when the food came.

TIP-TOP

My parents were poor, but they always tipped generously because they had compassion for other working people. This compassion does not always cross class lines. I attended a high-society wedding where private buses were hired to bring us from the church to the reception and then back to our hotel. When we got to our final destination, the host on our bus, the groom's brother—the scion of an old-money family—neglected to tip the driver. When someone (me) took him aside and suggested that a gratuity might be in order, his drunken response was something like, "Why? He's already been paid." So much for noblesse oblige.

Like I said, maybe it's a class thing. When I was in college, my roommate's boyfriend, Toby, got a summer job as a bellboy in a Catskills hotel. One weekend the hotel was taken over by a group of gentlemen who were there for an international business conference. The business was crime, and the gentlemen were Cosa Nostra. Toby never got less than a $100 tip for carrying bags. Well, that's only fair: Uzis are heavy.

YANKEE-PANKY

Moneyed people are not the only ones who can be stingy. There was a little general store down the road from our country house. George, the owner, never turned on the lights in order to save money, a good example of "penny wise, pound foolish." Needless to say, business was not booming. Not too many people want to poke around in the dark for a dusty can of baked beans from 1947.

One day I asked George if he would put aside the local paper for me each week. I wanted to be sure that it would not be sold out when we arrived on Fridays, since it contained the all-important auction and garage sale listings. George, with his sharp sense of business acumen, agreed to save the paper as long as I gave him the twenty-five cents in advance.

It might be a good idea to control those cheapskate instincts when you're out on a date. Ann Rita, an actress friend, met a guy online. They chatted a few times on the phone and finally agreed to get together for brunch. As they studied the menu, he suggested, "Why don't we just split an order of toast?" Ann Rita is not particularly materialistic, but she had to swallow the impulse to say, "Why don't you have the toast and I'll just split?"

ON THE HOUSE

The richer you are, the more freebies you command, from Oscar ceremony gowns to comped suites in Vegas. This is a two-way street: The dress designer wants his label to be seen, and the hotel figures they'll make the room fee back, and more, at the blackjack table. But it's not just celebs who expect freebies.

When I do my solo shows, I am amazed at how many people expect to be given tickets. Of course, you have to comp agents, casting people, and the press. But then there are folks who crawl out of the woodwork, like the distant acquaintance who requested that I comp him because he wrote online reviews. I promised him a ticket, and he asked if I could make it two. He brought a bimbo date, he never wrote a review, and I had to cover the cost of the two seats. On the other hand, I offered Oscar winner Estelle Parsons freebies, which she graciously turned down, saying that she wanted to support the theater. Some folks have class.

> The lead actor in a Broadway megahit had a milestone birthday. The cast and crew had to chip in for a cake because the producers refused to pay for it.

Bob Hope was generous with his time and talent, but he was also a notorious tightwad. When he invited his writers to his house for a brainstorming session, he advised them in advance to bring their own orange juice.

ALL IN THE FAMILY

The worst cheapskates are people who are stingy with their own families.

- Peter, a real estate mogul, refused to give his son a college graduation present, saying, "I don't believe in buying affection." As it turned out, the kid had secretly dropped out of school to do drugs, but still.

- Sally's father was a wealthy entrepreneur. When he died, he left his estate to any future grandchildren; if there were no grandchildren, the money would go to an animal charity. Sally was forty-four and her sister was fifty-two, both unmarried and childless. As it turned out, Sally met a guy and had a daughter at the age of forty-five. She dearly loves her child, but sometimes I think she got pregnant just to spite dear old Dad.

- My Danish father-in-law, Harry, was a lawyer married to a society woman. Their wedding present to us was a little tablecloth and a pair of pewter candlesticks. My own father, a poor immigrant tailor, gave us $2,000. I still managed to squeeze a little cash out of Harry. Whenever I saw him, I would say, "Oh, gee, I forgot my wallet. Could I borrow 100 Kroner?" Harry was your typically reserved Scandinavian, so I knew he would be too polite to ever ask for the money back. Yes, I am a shameless whore, but cheapskates need to be brought to justice.

A theater producer had agreed to mount one of my shows. He suggested that Benni and I meet him for lunch to go over the contract, and he named the restaurant. At the end of the meal, not only did Mr. Producer not pick up the check, but he divided it into three and paid his third. I should have known then that it would be a mistake doing business with this guy. Ten years after the production, he still owes us money.

CHEAP-ISH

Like everyone else, the wealthy have their peculiarities. I wouldn't really call them cheap—just eccentric.

- Helen Gurley Brown always brought a brown-bag lunch to her office. In a way, I admire her frugality, although I suspect that someone else made the lunch for her.

- Supreme Court Justice Souter, a multimillionaire, is retiring to a shabby New Hampshire farmhouse that has peeling paint, sagging windows, and a rusty mailbox. The landscaping consists of five daffodils.

- Warren Buffett does not carry a cell phone, does not have a computer at his desk, and drives his own automobile. This great philanthropist's home in Omaha is less imposing than any of "The Real Housewives'" faux palazzos.

$3 Extreme Cases

Paul, a film director, is an old friend of Benni's. Paul made a pile of money many years ago and bought a nice hilltop house in Topanga Canyon, which is a Woodstock-like area outside of Los Angeles. Eventually, the money ran out. Paul's show-biz opportunities had dwindled, since he was over twenty-five. So with his own two hands he built a smaller home on his property, which he moved into. He rents out the big house, which gives him enough income to live on if he is very frugal. And that he is.

He has a huge garden in which he grows all his food. He rolls his own pasta, bakes his own bread, and sews his own clothes. By living this way, he saves enough money for European vacations, like going to the Wagner festival in Bayreuth, Germany. This sounds more like a punishment than a reward to me.

Paul enjoys being a host, and he gives big parties where each guest gets a gift bag of freshly picked tomatoes, zucchini, and salad greens from his mini-farm. We are also invited to swim in the pond that he, needless to say, dug out himself.

SOMEWHERE, UNDER THE RADAR

My friend Mimi lives very happily without a credit card, a cell phone, or a dishwasher. She also doesn't have a computer or cable TV, so she's not very plugged in to pop culture. One night a big, hulking guy rang the bell of her Greenwich Village studio and begged her to do a portrait of his dying dog. She was busy with other commissions and didn't think she could find the time, but the guy was desperate and offered twice her usual fee.

The next day, she went to photograph the dog and was chatting with the client's wife, who said how hard it was for them to go out in public because her husband was always recognized. Mimi called me afterward. "Have you ever heard of an actor named James Gandolfini? I think he's on some HBO show about the Mafia."

GOING MONASTIC

I read a *New York Times* article about some dedicated folks who have joined the voluntary simplicity movement. They feel that "everything you own owns you." They unburden themselves of material possessions and try to live a simple, spiritual, sustainable existence.

- One family lives in an RV powered by vegetable oil and motors across the county living on $1,500 a month.

- A couple emptied their apartment at an "everything must go" party. Their home is now a forty-four- by twenty-four-foot catamaran.

- Another couple donated all their belongings to charity and hope to become organic homesteaders in Vermont.

I'm all for simplicity, but this Spartan lifestyle seems extreme. I'd love to be a fly on the wall when the kids of these Nouveau Puritans become teenagers and learn what they've been missing. "I just went to Tommy's house, and they have this really cool thing called television!"

Some environmentalists are reducing their carbon foot-prints by getting rid of their refrigerators. This would not work for us: Benni is Danish, which means he needs to have a cold beer handy at all times.

Success Story

Our friend Danny Klein was not destined for success. As a matter of fact, when he got into Harvard, his father thought it was a fluke and wrote to the dean of admissions (with the central-casting name of F. Skiddy von Stade) expressing his concerns. Danny's older brother was a math and science genius, but Papa Klein feared that his younger son was too "whimsical" to do well at this great university.

Danny majored in philosophy, not a subject likely to lead to riches. He managed to graduate and then spent many years exploring the "whimsical" side of life, as in sex, drugs, and rock 'n' roll. Eventually, he settled down and became a writer. He has done nonfiction, mysteries, serious novels, ghostwriting, whatever came his way, including a few board games, the occasional TV script, and several unproduced screenplays. Danny never made much money from these projects, but was always content with his lot.

He and his journalist wife live on a country road in the Berkshires, where they raised a lovely daughter. Danny enjoys a warm circle of friends and often takes European trips on the really really cheap, like traveling at night and sleeping on the train to save the cost of a hotel room.

It's been an adventurous life, but a precarious one, and Danny's more practical wife constantly worried about their lack of financial security. Danny's answer to her fears was always, "Don't worry, something will turn up." Then Danny was hit with some serious medical problems, and even he had to acknowledge that things were looking bleak. So he did what he's always done in the face of adversity: He decided to have some fun.

He got together with an old Harvard classmate, and they decided to write a book that combined humor and philosophy. The book was called *Plato and a Platypus Walk into a Bar* . . . It was rejected by forty publishers. Danny switched to my agent, Julia, who got it sold. Two weeks after the book hit the stores, it was number three on the *New York Times* best seller list. It became an international success, and the third volume in the series brought an advance of half a million dollars. Of course, Danny couldn't resist saying to his wife, "See? I told you something would turn up!"

I just wish Danny's father had been around to see that "whimsical" isn't necessarily a bad thing.

Last Words

PART

VII

$1 Pop Quiz: Are You a True Bargainista?

These questions will test your thriftyhood. (Hint: The correct answer is always B.)

1. You are about to leave a restaurant, and there is still some bread left in the basket. You

   A. are not at all agonized by the thought that it will all be dumped into the garbage.

   B. wrap the remaining slices in a napkin for tomorrow's breakfast. This is why you always carry a large bag.

2. You see a quarter lying on the sidewalk. You

   A. walk on by without sullying your fingers.

   B. bend down, pick it up, put it in your pocket, and hand it to the next homeless person you come across.

3. You bring home a pound of potato salad from an overpriced deli. At dinner, you discover that the potatoes are sorely undercooked. You

   A. force it down, pretending that the crunchiness comes from carrots.

   B. return it the next day and demand a refund, which you use on something safe like a jar of chopped sun-dried tomatoes.

4. Your friend is moving out of town and offers you two huge boxes of kitchenware. You do not like or need any of it. You

A. politely refuse, explaining that you have limited storage space.

B. gratefully accept and then sell it all at your next garage sale.

5. The restaurant charges an extra $7.95 to add a salad buffet to your steak dinner. You and your husband

A. both pay the additional charge.

B. get just one buffet and let the other person have a few little tastes.

And I do mean "little." Otherwise it's stealing. This way it's only stealing a teensky-weensky bit. I once got nailed—unfairly, I thought—for a similar attempt on an airplane. Benni had heroically offered me all his miles, so I was traveling first class, and he was stuck in economy. His only request was that I bring him a mimosa.

When the steward offered drinks, I felt it would be chintzy to ask for two, so I only took one and brought it back to Hubby. I was severely chastised by the attendant, who said that it was unfair for my spouse to receive a free drink when the people around him had to pay. I failed to see the logic of this one but offered to bring back more drinks for Benni's seat-mates. The attendant was not amused.

You, Too, Can Earn Money at Home

We've all seen those TV ads that scream, "Work at home! Earn thousands of dollars a week!" If you believe them, I've got a bridge I'd like to sell you. However, it is true that you can fatten your income at home, and not just by playing online poker. All you need is a phone, a computer, and a little ingenuity. You can buy and sell like Benni and I do, or there are other options.

- Benni's friend Ron was a TV director who hit the gray ceiling. In desperation, he took a telemarketing job for an outfit that sold computer supplies. It was the worst day of his life. As it turned out, Ron enjoyed schmoozing with people on the phone, and he became a crackerjack salesman. He decided to leave the company and strike out on his own. He set up a computer supply business in his garage, which was so successful that he ended up employing five people.

- Richard has helped me develop my solo shows. He is the artistic director of a small nonprofit theater company. This is an exhilarating job that brings in zero bucks. To support his theater addiction, Richard types legal transcripts at home. He can set his own hours and is able to live in modest comfort while enjoying life on the boards.

- I met Tricia at a party. She told me she used to walk a neighbor's frisky dog as a favor. People heard about how well she handled this pooch and asked if they could pay her to take care of their dogs. Sometimes Tricia is asked to move in and dog-sit while the owners are out of town. She took some classes to expand her dog-handling skills and now has a part-time pet nanny business that brings in $1,000 a week.

- There's always phone sex, but you burn out pretty fast. I had one gay friend who did it, and he started to develop ear strain. The guys at the other end were always whispering because they didn't want their wives to hear them in the next room.

I Go on *Oprah,*
or, a Frugalista Regrets

$3

Oprah Winfrey is doing a show about "Ethnic Men Who Reject Their Own Women." I have been invited as an expert witness because I've been speaking and writing about the ugly stereotypes some Jewish men have created about their wives and mothers. Oprah flies me to Chicago, first-class. Big mistake.

You see, I'm such a compulsive frugalista that I've got this problem with food: If someone else is paying, and I can have whatever I want, I just lose all control. It's like there's this tape in my brain that keeps playing over and over from my childhood, "Finish your plate! Little children in Europe are starving!" My friend Sandra's mother used to say, "Eat whatever you want—and the rest put in your mouth!"

So I'm on the plane, and the chirpy attendant says, "Hi there! For your hors d'oeuvre, would you care for smoked salmon, artichoke dip, or pâté?" I say yes to all three, which I follow with a stuffed Cornish game hen and a hot fudge sundae. I wobble off the plane, and a limo whisks me to my luxurious hotel, just in time for dinner. Oprah Winfrey is trying to kill me.

I don't feel so good. All my body really wants is a nice cup of chamomile tea, but I tell my body to mind its own business, and I sit down to a five-course dinner with beef stroganoff. (I don't usually eat red meat, but it's the most expensive thing on the menu.) My body is very angry with me. I just hope those little children in Europe are happy!

I am seriously unwell. I can't sleep. What am I going to say on the show tomorrow? How can I convince people that Jewish women deserve some respect? At 5:30 I get a wake-up call. I'm sicker than ever, but breakfast arrives. I force down eggs Benedict and a stack of buttermilk pancakes. What choice do I have? It's paid for! At 6:30, the limo arrives to take me, green and nauseous, to the studio. It's showtime!

The first speaker is a single Jewish professional man, and he spouts the usual garbage: "I never date Jewish women. They look alike, they think alike, the only thing they're interested in is the size of your wallet!"

It's my turn to reply, and I want to bury this jerk with my cutting wit and irresistible charm. But by now there are clumps of Stroganoff in Benedict sauce floating around in my esophagus, and I am about to represent Jewish women by vomiting in front of 22 million people. I am so sick that my witty and charming response is "Same to you and double!" And then I gag.

The next day, at home, Benni feels my pain and makes a lame attempt to console me. "Don't worry about it. Who watches *Oprah* anyway?" Jonathan saves face by going around telling all his friends that I'm not really his mother; he's adopted. You know the expression, "There's no such thing as a free lunch?" I guess it's true.

$4 Drawbacks to the Frugalista Lifestyle

IS FRUGALISM UNPATRIOTIC?

I've been cautioned that if everyone followed my bargain junkie philosophy, it would be a disaster for global commerce. Not at all. I have no fears of causing yet another economic meltdown, for the simple reason that compulsively thrifty living is not for everyone. You have to be very disciplined, very patient, and a little bit cuckoo to live as I do.

For one thing, there's not a whole lot of instant gratification. I rarely buy things when I want them. I rarely buy things when I need them. I buy things when I come across them at the right price. This means I often have to delay pleasure.

Years ago, I lost an audiocassette of one of my favorite country singers, K. T. Oslin. Two months ago, I found the CD at a yard sale for one dollar. Most people would not have waited a decade to replace the cherished album, but, then again, most people never experience the rush of suddenly discovering a long-yearned-for item for a buck.

I don't always find what I want, and I'm willing to accept that. Suffering is a part of life, and I am tortured by my living room curtains. Actually, they're not curtains, they are formal, pleated, lifeless beige grandma drapes. Actually, they're not just in the living room, they're also in the dining room. They came with the house rental, and I didn't have the foresight to remove them immediately, before we painted. Now I seem to be stuck with them. That's because I cannot face the expense and the ordeal of:

- Having new curtains custom-made for six extra-long, extra-wide windows

- Removing the old pulley system

- Replacing the hardware

- Patching and repainting the walls

None of this can be done on the cheap. Believe me, I've tried: I have bought boxes and boxes of beautiful window treatments that turn out to be the wrong width, the wrong length, the wrong type, whatever. A normal person would just spend a few thousand dollars and get the job done. I prefer to keep complaining about the boring drapes and filling my linen closet with gorgeous but useless curtains.

There are other reasons my second-hand lifestyle is not for everyone.

- Some folks would rather do without lunch tomorrow than be seen carrying a doggy bag out of a restaurant.

- The majority of people won't wear used clothing. Some of this aversion has to do with hygiene. I wash garments before I wear them, and I wipe down shoe interiors with an astringent, but most folks are comfortable only in crisp, fresh, new stuff. And I hope they stay that way, because then I can get their cast-offs.

- If it's important to flaunt the sexiest car, the trendiest shades, the very latest Jimmy Choos, then you couldn't live my life. I do own Jimmy sandals and Armani sunglasses, but they were two years old when I bought them, and I've worn them for three years. Also, parking at a tag sale in a Lamborghini convertible would not be helpful during price negotiations. A bargainista needs to keep a low profile.

Wasteland

One of the most disturbing moments in any film is when Gloria Stuart flings the priceless blue diamond necklace into the water at the end of *Titanic*. I know we're supposed to be moved by that extravagant, romantic gesture. Instead, thriftaholic that I am, I am horrified by the reckless wastefulness. So you can imagine how challenging it is for someone like me to live in our disposable culture. Here are just a few of my pet peeves.

- Throw-away cigarette lighters were invented by Satan.

- You are given a tall glass of water in a restaurant before asking for it, and it is surreptitiously refilled all night long, even in drought-prone places like Los Angeles.

- Theater programs are glanced at once, then thrown in the trash. (I always return mine to the usher.)

- You buy five pairs of socks and come home with five useless plastic hanger gizmos, which go right into the garbage unless you happen to have a hanging-sock closet

- I'd like to do away with paper plates, paper napkins, and plastic utensils. It's cheaper, greener, and a lot more inviting to use pretty dishes, flatware, and linens that you pick up at tag sales. Plus, wine tastes a lot better in a real glass than in a paper or plastic cup, even to my underdeveloped palate. True, you have to wash everything afterwards, but that's what spouses, partners, kids, and best friends are for.

RUNNING HOT AND COLD

Excessive climate control makes me nuts. I resent having to bring a sweater to the movies in July and then sweltering in a department store in December. It's time to scale back on these not-so-comfortable "comforts." I will admit I feel differently if I'm in a stifling heat wave in France. Europeans think air conditioning is something only used by spoiled Americans. They even sneered when I asked for some ice in my drink. Let me tell you something, Mr. Fancypants Euro-man: On a scorching summer day, a lukewarm Campari and soda doesn't really do the trick.

I was having problems with my microphone and asked a sound technician if I needed to buy a new one. He was shocked. He explained that he was from India, where people do not throw things away, and he offered to repair the mic for me. He did, and I've been getting good use from it ever since. Maybe more of us should share his "don't-toss-it-just-yet" philosophy.

ROOM DISSERVICE

Hotels can be criminally wasteful.

- Every towel is washed, bleached, and dried after one day's use.

- The air-conditioning is left on all day, even in empty rooms.

- Empty mini-fridges are running constantly.

- A raging waterfall blasts out of the shower.

The worst offenders are in Vegas. I love Steve Wynn, and I love the over-the-top fabulousness of his hotels, but I think his next venture should be an eco-friendly place called The Palace Green and yes, Steve, I will happily accept comps for the opening weekend.

No country is as lavish as we are with electric lights. We just leave them burning all the time. In Europe, when you enter a restroom you turn on the light, and when you leave—guess what?—you turn it off. So simple!

I'm a member of the Screen Actors Guild. Every month my union sends me a thick, colorful, glossy magazine that consists mostly of photographs of union delegates at union functions. The rare item of interest could easily and cheaply be transmitted in an e-mail. So my dues are being spent on ink, paper, postage, and editorial salaries for this useless publication, money that could certainly be put to better use. How about an annual Caribbean holiday for older, ethnic character actresses?

And then there's the packaging nightmare. So much of what we buy is wrapped to kill. I bought some low-fat Jarlsberg cheese at Whole Foods that was encased in a plastic container so thick I had to use a hammer and chisel to bust it open. I prefer the old-fashioned neighborhood deli (if you can find one) where they slice the cheddar onto a piece of waxed paper, which I use again to wrap half-used tomatoes.

WHEN I'M IN CHARGE

Of course, our biggest waste-monger is the government. I would
like to suggest a new cabinet post: Secretary of Frugality. Please note
that I am available for the job. Here are the first few items I would
deal with.

- I volunteered to be a poll worker on Election Day and was obliged
  to take a two-hour training class. We were each handed three
  thick volumes of instructions. My particular job description took
  up half a page. I wonder what amount of trees and water and oil
  were wasted in order to print thousands of those useless instruction books

- Actors collect unemployment between jobs. While I was on
  the dole, I frequently received letters from the Unemployment
  Department inviting me to learn job skills as a metalworker.
  I wonder how many thousands of these notices were sent out. I
  wonder how much paper, energy, and labor was wasted. I wonder
  how many actors seek training as metalworkers.

- I will permanently abolish the automatic flush toilet, a truly
  diabolical invention. The airport restroom sounds like Niagara
  Falls. The automatic gizmo is so sensitive that it flushes when you
  look at it, flushes when you sit down, flushes while you do your
  business, and flushes again to say bye-bye. I may be technologically
  challenged, but I am perfectly capable of pulling a toilet handle.
  I wonder how many millions of gallons of precious water are
  squandered by a totally unnecessary "convenience." Why don't they
  invent something useful instead, like an electronic eyeglass locator?

223

- Our primitive, brutal, congested penal system has got to be one of the biggest money-wasters around, along with that insane "War on Drugs." I say make more drugs legal—in addition to alcohol and nicotine—then tax the hell out of them and use that money to educate and empower those young people who are looking to escape their hopeless lives. They will then get good jobs, buy nice homes, and get high on things that we respectable people are addicted to, like crispy baguettes and *30 Rock*. Again, it's so simple!

When I am Secretary of Frugality, I promise to:

- Turn garbage into mulch

- Turn bath water into garden water

- Turn cooking oil into fuel

- And let those windmills turn

CAUTIOUS OPTIMISM

I believe Americans are capable of change, and there are small signs of progress.

- In my own profession, actors used to have to print out pictures and résumés by the hundreds. Now many casting people use a barcode system—no glossies necessary.

- Also, instead of driving across town to pick up a script, the material is now sent by e-mail—no gasoline necessary.

- Many hotels now give you the choice of keeping your slightly used towels instead of automatically laundering them.

- I attended a school concert recently, and the programs were printed on scrap paper.

   Hope springs eternal!